**Gerald Benedict** graduated in Divinity from the University of London, and has a postgraduate diploma from the Graduate School of Ecumenical Studies, University of Geneva, and a PhD from the Open University. He held a commission with the Royal Marines, serving in Sierra Leone with the Royal West African Frontier Force. His main academic interest is comparative religious philosophy, and after teaching religious studies and philosophy in colleges and universities in Britain, he moved to France. He is the author of the *Watkins Dictionary of Religions and Secular Faiths* and *Celtic Wisdom* in the Sacred Texts series, both published by Watkins Publishing, and he has won awards for a novel, several short stories, and radio drama for the BBC World Service.

By the Same Author


*The Mayan Prophecies 2012 - the Message and the Vision*
*The Mayan Prophecies for 2012* (HB)
*Watkins Dictionary of Religions and Secular Faiths*
Sacred Texts: *Celtic Wisdom*
Sacred Texts: *The Song of Songs and the Psalms*
Sacred Texts: *Buddhism*
Sacred Texts: *Chinese Wisdom*

# THE MAYAN PROPHECIES
## FOR
## 2012

### GERALD BENEDICT

WATKINS PUBLISHING

LONDON

First published in hardback in the UK in 2008 by
Watkins Publishing, Sixth Floor, Castle House,
75–76 Wells Street, London W1T 3QH

This edition first published 2011
Reprinted 2011

3 5 7 9 10 8 6 4 2

Designed and typeset by Jerry Goldie

Printed in India by Imago

British Library Cataloguing-in-Publication Data Available

ISBN: 978-1-907486-11-1

www.watkinspublishing.co.uk

# CONTENTS

APPENDICES: THE CALENDARS

*For my wife, Nadège,*

the still point of my turning world.

*Only may there be peace
in your presence.*

A Mayan blessing

# ACKNOWLEDGEMENTS

Many thanks are due to my editor, Michael Mann, for the wise counsel and guidance given throughout the writing of the book. He might well be a Chilam, himself. While I've been sky-watching, Penny Stopa has kept my feet on earth; Shelagh Boyd's sharp eye for detail would have served the Mayan astronomers well, as would her gentle advice and suggestions. Thanks are due to my wife, Nadège, for her clear thinking, and for redressing my innumeracy with her talent for mathematics. I am hugely grateful to my daughter Noémie for rescuing us with her Calendar Round image (p. 209).

I am indebted to Roeland Looff for his permission to quote from his website at: http://www.astrologycourse.org

Duncan M Roads, editor of the interesting and challenging *Nexus New Times*, gave permission to quote from Vol. 14, No 3, April–May 2007, and Vol. 10, Number 3 (April–May 2003) http://www.nexusmagazine.com

Jacob Rhythmic Dragon, Director of Communications at the Foundation for the Law of Time (http://www.lawoftime.org), offered indispensable guidance on the Telektonon Prophecy, the quotations from which are rendered and transcribed by Dr José Argüelles/Valum Votan, to whom, sincere thanks.

Eden Sky was enthusiastic and encouraging in allowing me to use material about Pacal Votan from his website http://www.13moon.com .

David A Dundee, astronomer, and Director and Chairman of the Fernbank Science Centre Planetarium, rescued me from outer space by allowing material to be used concerning planetary conjunctions for 2012, specifically with regard to the winter equinox.

NASA were kind enough to respond to my questions about sunspot activity and changes in the Earth's magnetic field during 2012.

I have made every effort to secure permission to reproduce material protected by copyright, and will be pleased to make good any omissions brought to my attention in future printings of this book.

Note: Endnotes are listed in the References section, and ˃ indicates Further Reading.

# THE MAYA REGIONS & MAJOR SITES

Tizimin

Dzibalchaltún

**Mérida** ■ ▲ Ixil    Chichén    Ek Balam
Oxintok ▲             Itzá ▲

▲ Mayapan    ▲ Mani

Uxmal ▲         ▲ Kaua    Tulum ▲
Chumayel

Yucatán

*Northern Lowlands*

*Gulf of*
*Campeche*

Quintana
Roo

Campeche

**MEXICO**

Tabasco

Calakmul ▲

*Central Lowlands*

Nah Chan ▲
(Palenque)

Piedras        ▲ Tikal
Negras

Toniná ▲                              **BELIZE**
**San Cristóbal**    Yaxchilán ▲
**de las Casas**                ▲ Tayasal
Bonampak ▲ •Frontera de
Corazal

Chiapas                           Lubaantún
                                      ▲

*Caribbean Sea*

**GUATEMALA**

Izapa                **Chichicastenango**              **HONDURAS**
▲
Iximché ▲ ▲ Mixco Viejo
**Antigua** ■   ▲ Copán
           **Guatemala**    *Southern Mountains*
           **City**

**EL SALVADOR**

0        100 km

*Prophecy is not prediction, even though it purports to be so. Prophecy is a thread in the total fabric of meaning, in the total world-view. In this way it can be seen as a way of life and of being.*

Armin Geertz

*The Mayan prophecies are being fulfilled. Some are being fulfilled even now. Some will be fulfilled on the morrow. The Mayan prophecies exist because the Maya knew the cosmic time. They knew that in certain times it would be necessary to keep this cosmic wisdom secret. This was the purpose of the prophecy so that they might be able to communicate their secrets to the initiates of the future.*

Hunbatz Men

*Wisdom is knowing in depth the great metaphors of meaning.*

C G Jung

# THE MAYA – AN OVERVIEW

The Maya have a holistic understanding of the spirit, the soul, the gods, human beings and numbers (or mathematics). It is from the subtle integration of these that their calendars were constructed and the energies for prophecy derived.

Regardless of everything scientists have learned about the Maya so far, we constantly encounter unanswered questions. No one has satisfactorily explained where or when Maya civilization originated, or how it evolved in an environment so hostile to human habitation. We have no reliable information on the origin of their calendar, hieroglyphic writing, and mathematical system; nor do we understand countless details pertaining to their socio-political organization, religion, economic structure, and everyday life. Even the shattering catastrophe leading to the sudden abandonment of their greatest cities during the 9th century CE – one of the most baffling archaeological mysteries uncovered – is still deeply shrouded in conjecture.[1]

## A WORD ABOUT 'PROPHECY'

The word 'prophecy' is used in several different ways. In the traditional concept, derived from the Old Testament, the prophet was 'called out', by God, to deliver a specific message at a special time to a particular people. Such a prophet would have been a person of impeccable religious and moral character fulfilling God's conditions of righteousness. In general, the prophet's message was one of warning; he spoke of the future in terms of what the consequences would be if the people continued to flaunt God's laws and failed to change their ways. The prophet Jeremiah received the message directly, as when God told him, '*I put my words into your mouth*' (Jeremiah 1:5–8 Tanakh˃). Isaiah volunteered, '*Here am I; send me*' (Isaiah 6:4–8 Tanakh˃). Ezekiel received the message he was to carry somewhat dramatically, '*the heavens opened and I saw visions of God*' (Ezekiel 1:1 Tanakh˃). In such ways was the authority of the prophet established, he 'went out' with his message and described how the future of the people he spoke to would be determined by their behaviour and the choices they made.

In more popular usage, the word 'prophecy' means making known what will happen in the future regardless of how we behave. There is little, or nothing, we can do to change the course of events, and our most positive response is to be prepared. Such a prophet was the 16th-century Provençal Frenchman, Nostradamus, who according to one interpreter,[2] foretold (among many other events) the recent great flood of New Orleans, global warming, and the future abdication of Charles III of England. The prophecies of Edgar Cayce (1877–1945) are in the same vein; out of a self-induced trance, Cayce has prophesied the raising of Atlantis, the destruction of California, Earth changes, pole shifts and the Second Coming of Christ. Beyond these forms of prophecy are those better referred to as predictions or divinations which in classical antiquity were associated with oracles and, throughout history, with astrology.

All these forms of prophecy can be found within the Mayan tradition; however, one very important element has to be added. The authority of 'true' prophecy lies not just in the sources inspiring the prophet, but in the extent to which it adds new insight to the received tradition of revelation. In this case the power of the prophecy goes beyond its apparent character of warning, and gives direction as to how spiritual maturity can be advanced; such a prophecy elicits responses to its message that are both practical and transcendent. The Mayan prophecies achieve this, especially those now communicated by contemporary Mayan day-keepers and elders such has Hunbatz Men. The Mayan prophecies both alert us to the huge changes we are about to face, and at the same time enhance our spiritual awareness. So completely is the whole notion of prophecy embedded in Mayan culture and way of life, that it can be thought of as their spiritual DNA.

## ORIGINS

The Maya are not bygone, vanished people, and their present population runs to about six million; among them are those who continue to maintain the ancient calendric traditions and practices. Their origin, however, is obscure and the issue continues to be debated by scholars. Of the more imaginative, but beguiling, theories is the possibility of their descent from survivors of Atlantis; another refers to ancient migrations across the Bering land-bridge at the end of the last ice age. More plausible is their development from the Olmec, who inhabited the coastland regions of Vera Cruz and Tabasco. Evidence for this is based on a common mythology of the god Kukulcan, who may have been an actual person, such as a wise and beneficent king. It is thought that during the early and middle pre-Classical period, c.1000–300 BCE, the myth of Kukulcan was carried by migrants and traders to the Mayan regions of Yucatan and Guatemala. However, current research suggests that Mayan roots were spread wider than the Olmec, and that a melding of many different influences is more likely.

As we know them, the Maya are a short, dark-skinned Amerindian people with straight black hair, a characteristic feature being the roundness of their heads. They speak a large number of languages and dialects developed from a single proto-Mayan language that was in use prior to 2000 BCE. From this early date, and from among a people who were roaming hunters, the Maya eventually established an agriculture that required permanent settlement. It was from this simple, agrarian, base that one of the most sophisticated civilizations in Mesoamerica evolved, being the first to develop writing, mathematics and an extraordinary knowledge of astronomy, and to construct massive public ceremonial architecture.

## GEOGRAPHY & AGRICULTURE

In and around 1540 CE, at the time of the Spanish conquest, the Maya occupied Guatemala, British Honduras (now Belize), and El Salvador; in Mexico they inhabited the regions of Yucatan, Campeche, Quintana Roo, most of Tabasco and eastern Chiapas. The territories are geographically and climatically diverse, ranging from snow-covered volcanoes to lowland plains, from tropical rainforests to arid deserts. These regions naturally divide into three distinguishable areas.

- The southern mountains of Guatemala and western El Salvador, featuring volcanoes, canyons and a temperate climate.
- The central lowland areas, including the southern half of the Yucatan peninsula. This is a region of hot tropical forest and heavy rainfall.
- The northern part of the Yucatan peninsula, which is a region of porous limestone from which the topsoil has been eroded, and where the rivers and lakes were formed underground. Here there is less rain, and what soil remains is superficial, the rock is exposed and the great forest gives way to rough scrub.

The Mayan civilization with which we are concerned flourished on the immense lowland, limestone shelf forming the Petén-Yucatan peninsula that thrusts out into the Gulf of Mexico. Here the climate is hot, and in the south very wet during the rainy season of May to October. The northern region of the peninsula is much drier, requiring the Maya to 'excavate and construct thousands of underground, bottle-shaped cisterns'.[3] Critical was the agriculture developed on the lowlands at the expense of forest clearing, reminiscent of the 'slash and burn' techniques used today in the Amazon; each cleared area was viable for only two or three years. These, they planted with maize on a shifting, rather than fixed-field method. Recent research indicates that the clearance method was supplemented by a raised-field system supported by stone walls in the form of terraces. The impression is given that maize was the dominant crop, but almost certainly they cultivated the *ramón*, or Brosimum tree for its breadnuts, but this may have been a famine-food to fall back on in hard times. Towards the end of the Classical period, it is estimated that Mayan agriculture was capable of sustaining a population of eight to ten million, a sizeable percentage of which were not farmers, but occupied with the practical and administrative skills on which their civilization was founded. The deterioration of the cleared land, and the consequent loss of agriculture may have been one of the reasons for the rapid decline of their civilization, and their sudden, mysterious, disappearance in the 9th century CE (*see below*).

## CULTURE & CIVILIZATION

Mayan culture, which combines a unique conjunction of gods, human beings and mathematics, was sufficiently distinctive to be called 'Mayan' by the beginning of the

Christian era. The civilization reached its apogee during what is termed, the 'Classical period', c.300–900 CE. It developed most fully in the central areas of the lowlands, responding to the natural challenges of the tropical forest. The highland Maya of Guatemala developed a rich and thriving economy, but played very little part in the development of the hieroglyphics, sculptures and architecture of their lowland cousins. The culture of the northern communities developed in parallel to their neighbours in the southern forests, but beyond the Classical period, marked regional differences became apparent.

The Maya were the only Mesoamerican people to evolve a form of writing that established a hieroglyphic 'alphabet' of around 850 characters. These were carved on steles, monuments, buildings, wood, jade and shells, and inscribed in codices of which only a very few have survived. They are renowned for their achievements in mathematics, especially as applied to astronomy, but how they came by this knowledge is as much an anthropological mystery as their origin. Eventually, they were able to predict eclipses of the Sun, but not which of these would be visible to them; they did not know that the Moon revolved around the world, or the world around the Sun. They calculated the average synodical revolution of Venus with great accuracy (*see* Prophecy 9) an error amounting to just 1 day in 6,000 years. It is this extraordinary knowledge of mathematics and astronomy that is the raw material of the Mayan calendars, the most important of which are fully described and illustrated in the Appendices. The architecture was as striking as that of ancient Egypt, and not without similarities, but they were unable to develop a true arch, using instead, the corbelled form; both the buildings, and their disposition on the ground are constructed models of planetary constellations. The pyramids were surmounted by temples, some of which were as much as 200 feet above ground level, and decorated with the low-relief sculpture that has survived as one the world's great art forms, as has their lapidary work in jade. Because the Maya had no metal, beans of the cacao tree were used as currency during the Classical period.

The Maya artificially deformed the heads of babies to produce a steeply sloped forehead. The reasons given for simulating this simian effect range from their interest in snakes to the belief that the shape mimicked that of an earlier aristocratic class. As did other primitive people, they filed their teeth, and tattooed and scarified their bodies as a form of decoration. They had many ways of disposing of the dead, and their death and burial practices were an important aspect of their religion. They both respected and feared death, grieving for the deceased. Maize was placed in the mouth of the dead as a symbol of rebirth, and jade, or stone beads were added as currency to pay for the spirit's journey. The corpse was wrapped in cotton, and as the colour red was symbolic of both death and rebirth, either the body or the grave was covered with cinnabar. Several extravagantly decorated and furnished tombs have been found, thought to be the burial place of kings or city rulers. Mathematics was the key skill, both in recording astronomic data and in the construction of the calendars; unlike our Western, decimal metric form, the system is vigesimal, that is, based on a computation of 20.

It is thought that they were among the first to use the concept of zero, which is represented by the image of a formalized shell 🐚 or sometimes a flower; one was marked by a dot •, five by a line or bar, ▬ . Thus, the numbers were built up to give, for example, three •••, ten ▬▬, and thirteen ▬▬••• . In the codices and on steles, etc., the numbers were displayed vertically, their value increasing from bottom to top. Twenty was represented by the glyph for the Moon, and sometimes in the codices numbers were represented by 'portrait variants', that is, the heads of deities. In Mayan cosmogony, all numbers had symbolic meanings and, inevitably, they were all interlinked. Such is the centrality of number and mathematics, that it was built in to the Mayan concept of an absolute god called, Hunab K'u, 'Sole God', the giver of movement and measure. (*see below*, Religion and Mythology).

While we have every reason to be in awe of what the Maya achieved in terms of mathematics, astronomy, art and architecture, there is one 'culture shock' issue that needs to be considered. The Maya practised an excessive and cruel form of human sacrifice in which children featured significantly. It is necessary to understand this within their own world-view and accept that, for them, it was a vital and sustaining aspect of their existence. Some anthropologists argue that the barbarous practice was fundamental to maintaining harmony. One primary source suggesting this, is the Quiché Maya's *Popol Vuh*,[4] which tells of the gods creating the human race as a source from which they would be supplied with nourishment in the form of sacrifice and prayer. Bonewitz[5] asks, '*Why were particular astronomical conditions seen as so dangerous that they needed the offering of human life to prevent some dreadful occurrence?*' He suggests that for the Maya, Venus was associated with a disaster of such huge proportions that only human sacrifice might prevent its recurrence (*see* Prophecy 9). Sacrifice, of course, takes many forms, but all of them symbolize the offering of the self. Put simply, human beings were vicariously sacrificed to the gods as reimbursement for the gift of life.

One ritual form of human sacrifice was the New Fire ceremony, practised to initiate a new Calendar Round (*see* Appendix 3) or, as a termination ceremony, on the last month of the year. As part of the ritual:

> ... all pots were smashed and new ones were

prepared for the new era. All fires were extinguished and the land lay in darkness awaiting the New Fire ceremony that confirmed and renewed the new year. ... At midnight before the first day of the new year, on a nearby mountain called Citlaltepec ('The Hill of the Star'), priests watched the movement of the stars we call the Pleiades. ... If they passed overhead at midnight, then the fire priests proceeded: they ripped out the heart of a sacrificial victim ... and started a flame with a fire drill in his open chest cavity.[5]

Life, for the Maya, was brutish and always at risk, and there was constant and urgent need to acknowledge the forces that were both life-giving and life-threatening. Time, as we shall see, was of the essence, and the notion of survival included not only borrowed time but time wrested or stolen from the gods as the prize of sacrifice.

## RELIGION & MYTHOLOGY

The Maya cultivated what was a highly developed form of nature religion. Essentially, this is a completely spontaneous response to the contemplation of, or sudden encounter with natural phenomena of the kind that evoke awe. This is sometimes combined with an overwhelming sense of mystery, the '*Mysterium Tremendum*', the numinous power of wonder, or dread. For the Maya, it takes the form of a holistic and intricate pantheism which understands everything that exists is bound by the same life force, or energy, thus a human being is an integral part of nature, inextricably related to Nature's creator. The mathematical intricacy and logic of the calendars is a visible and concrete form of this perception of nature.

The two outstanding features of Mayan religion are the concepts of unity, and replication:

**Unity** The gods, humans and numbers (or mathematics) are one and the same, representing a unity in plurality. Every multifarious aspect of nature fascinated the Maya who saw in the sky, earth and sea '*a dynamic and coherent whole*'.[6] The kind of unity characteristic of Mayan religion is not the monotheism of biblical religion; if one word could sum up the Mayan concept, it is the word 'energy'. A single, all-pervading energy is understood to support the entire observable universe, all natural phenomena and life. For the monotheistic, biblical religions this unified energy is understood as God. The name of the Mayan concept for the one, Absolute being is Hunab K'u, the source of movement and measurement, and on whom everything is dependent. The name means 'solitary' or 'sole' god', an epithet for the Maya's trend towards monotheism. An important distinction is made between the soul and the spirit. The soul is the *form* of the spirit, while spirit itself is energy. In Maya this is known as *K'inan*, from *K'in*, the Sun, and *an*, a conditional form of the verb 'to be'. Spirit is the Sun's being, or energy. The soul is a manifestation of the spirit, it is energy endowed with intelligence, temporally housed in a body. It is the soul that is understood as 'Measure', and the spirit as 'Movement'. In combination, what this amounts to is form and its vitalizing energy, the latter being the unifying principle.

**Replication** The concept of replication works both at a mundane and cosmic level. Patterns of everyday life are copied and cycled to form a map of fate, and the gods, together with their concerns and needs, were anthropomorphized to reflect cosmic geography. The human scale was copied into the cosmic, and the cosmic into the human. The Maya wanted to know who they were and where they were, and their experience of everything, from the cultivation of maize to calculating their location within cyclic time, was used in their search for an answer. Thus, their architecture also copied cosmic geography just as it did for the ancient Egyptians, the difference being that replication for the Maya meant establishing a human architecture that mirrored both its constructed and cosmic model.

The central Mayan creation myth is best represented in the *Popul Vuh* of the Quiché Maya, which tells of the gods, Tepeu and Gucumatz alone with the sea, enjoying their conversation; by means of their speech, creation is set in motion. That it is the 'word' that creates resonates with many other religious traditions. The account includes the important mythology of two sets of twins, one pair of which is sacrificed in the underworld, the other pair being the hero twins, the demon-slayers, talented at the ritual ball game played in the ball courts. The creation 'discussion' continues with the destruction of the wooden people and the creation of the maize people. This concept of sequences of destruction and creation suggests multiple creations, a characteristic of Mesoamerican mythology which is still current among the contemporary Maya.[7] The concept is also carried by the mythology of the world passing through five ages, or Five Suns, each ending with a destructive catastrophe before the 'New Age' is born. This is the cycle represented by the Long Count Calendar (*see* Appendix 4 and Prophecy 6).

The sudden arising of the earth in the midst of water has echoes of Babylonian mythology, which in turn influenced the more familiar account of creation in Genesis. The relationship and interdependence of earth and sky remains at the centre of Mayan religion and is significantly illustrated by the name of one their principal gods,

Quetzalcoatl. *Quetzal*, meaning a bird, and *coatl*, meaning snake, respectively a figure of the sky and the earth. It also represents a duality that belies the Mayan quest for harmony and balance. For the Maya, the balance or harmony of the individual with the community, nature, the world, the planets and the cosmos is not just a metaphor of health, economic prosperity and long life, but a condition of these. In contradistinction, imbalance and discord are associated with sickness, famine, even of world destruction. It is hard to resist both the individual and collective psychosomatic implication of this, that the Maya intuited that certain states of mind produce certain physical effects.

Mayan cosmology understands the world to be flat, but arranged in three familiar planes, the underworld, the sky, and the earth. The underworld, ruled over by Ah Puch, the god of death, was a place to be feared, but not a place of punishment as in the biblical concept of hell. It had 9 levels, represented in several 9-level pyramids, whereas the upper world had 13. The sky, a window in which the minds and activities of the star-associated gods could be observed, was ruled by the Sun and Itzamna, the Moon-god son of Hunab K'u. Thus, the constellations, their seasonal movements and intersections were observable phenomena that also told a story about the gods. It was the future, ongoing themes of this story that were communicated as prophecies to specialized priests called Chilans (*see below*).

The Maya supported a large pantheon of gods. They were not discrete and separate like the Greek gods, but entirely bound up with every aspect of human life. They *did not have a mythical concept of deities, but instead maintained that lords represented the forces of nature*.[8] Such were their attributes and affinities that they sometimes merged, as does the weather itself; gods might then represent Sun with rain, wind with thunder, sky in the form of low cloud and mist mingling with trees and hills. As with the Hindu pantheon, the gods are the manifestation of a single principle – for Hindus, Brahma, for the Maya, the consciousness of the one energy that pervades everything.[9] This considerable pantheon is thought to describe a mathematical representation of what was observed of nature. Each god was perceived as if it was a number, its function and effects seen, as noted above, in combination with the interaction of numbers represented in the calendars. Since Mayan culture developed to its highest point among the forest peoples, it is not surprising that the central deities were associated with growth and constant renewal. Among them were, the *Chacs*, the rain gods; the Moon, understood as the goddess of soil, birth and fertility; the Sun, and the maize god who provided the substance that was the basis of Mayan agricultural economy. The *Chacs*, like the other gods, were set in groups of four, each related to a cardinal point of the compass, and associated with one of four colours: white, yellow, red and black. Importantly, the Maya conceived of a fifth direction, that of the centre, which was omnipresent. Even as there is always an 'east', so there is always a centre. This centre was imagined as a huge tree, the ceiba tree, which connected the different planes of existence.

Of prime importance to the prophecies is the god Quetzalcoatl, referred to above. His name, in Yucatec Maya, is Kukulcan (*see* Prophecy 4). As a synthesis of bird and serpent, he is familiarly know in the West as 'the plumed serpent'. The *quetzal*, a bird that inhabits the cloud forest, is prized for its emerald-coloured feathers; the *coatl* is the rattlesnake. In the post-Classical period, Quetzalcoatl became the god of priests and merchants. Most importantly, the god, '*presides over another foundational act for the Mesoamerican peoples: the organization of time and space*'.[10] It is this organization, in the form of calendars and the prophecies based on them, that provides the theme of what follows.

## THE CALENDARS & THE MAYAN CONCEPT OF TIME

The prophecies, which are the principal concern of this book, are inextricably linked with the Mayan concept of time and the various ways this was recorded in the calendric cycles.

Our own received perception of time is of something that is entirely linear; it is assumed to have had a beginning, with perhaps the 'creation' of the world, and its conclusion, if conceived at all, is thought to be at some indeterminate point in the future. In Western culture, this linear view of time is derived from the Hebraic biblical account of creation. At the very moment God created a formless earth engulfed in darkness, time was set in motion. It was the Christianity of St Augustine that determined the end of time was to be marked by the second coming of Jesus Christ and the Day of Judgement. After that final moment, in some ethereal way, time will cease and if human life continues, it will do so in another dimension, traditionally referred to as 'eternity'. This religious view has, of course, been gradually secularized. The concept of time as having a beginning and an end gave way to one of time being formless, free of its traditional association with the planetary and astral movements, but somehow associated with the notion of progress, in terms of evolution, politics and economics. It is this linear concept of time that is made visible in the Gregorian calendar, and audible in the untold number of clocks and watches that inexorably tick time away. Whatever marks and measures time's replacement will not be in the form of calendars or clocks. The Mayan calendars offer an alternative to a linear concept of time, and one that is founded on their extraordinary knowledge of mathematics and astronomy.

Long before the inception of the Julian calendar, the

Maya developed numerous calendars of their own (*see* Appendices) and to understand the most important of these the Western mind has to make a considerable adjustment. One of the calendars does appear to have a linear form, representing time as duration, its forward motion measuring time passing, recording historical events, noting the present and enabling planning for the future (Appendix 4). However, we shall see that this familiar form of calendar is set in a conceptual context that is radically different from our own. More importantly, none of the basic calendars can be understood without considering its relationship to the others. They interlock, they are interdependent, their combination providing important insights and perceptions that would be missed if left unsynchronized and considered only individually.

It is thought that the Maya developed at least 20 calendric cycles, 17 of which are on record. Each of these had their dedicated association with, for example, the cycles of Venus, other planets, the Moon, the Sun, the Earth, the span of human life, rituals, and the organization and planning of agriculture and other daily activities. Most importantly, each calendar was the basis of divination and prophecy. Some of the calendars are thought to be extremely ancient and certainly those established by the Maya drew on earlier forms, for example those of the Olmec, which they inherited and perfected. For normal, everyday purposes, the Maya were bound by the linear aspect of time, but their calendars, and their religion and mythology, indicate they were conscious of what might be termed 'cosmic time'. They were mindful, as we are, of mortality, and yet their calendric systems leave us in no doubt they were aware of, and lived by the rhythms of the infinite.

In combination these calendars are complex, their raw material is advanced mathematics and an extraordinary knowledge of astronomy. The calendars are also comprehensive:

> It appears the Maya people once had differing
> systems of timekeeping for separate areas of their
> biological, astronomical, religious and social
> realities, and that these systems underwent a
> process of totalization within the overlapping,
> intermeshing cycles of their calendar.[11]

The calendars provided the framework out of which the prophecies themselves were given. The most important calendars are the Tun, the Tzolk'in, the Calendar Round, the Long Count Calendar, and those of the cycles of Venus, and the Tun Uc, the calendar of the Moon.

*A full account of these calendars is given in the Appendices.*

# THE PROPHETS & THEIR
# PROPHECIES

Prophecy for the Maya was not just a way of life, it was the ground of their being, the conceptual foundation of their mythology. Several elements combined to produce these prophecies; a class of specialized priests whose relationship with the gods gave them unique authority, the gods who imparted the prophecies, and the actual process of receiving and transmitting them. The prophecies cannot be interpreted and understood apart from the particular relationship that existed between religion, cosmology, astronomy, mathematics and spirituality. The priests transmitting the prophecies were mouthpieces, spokesmen, or interpreters and were highly regarded. They delivered the messages of the gods to the people, who carried them on their shoulders when they moved about. '*Priests*', says Chilam Balam of Tizimin, '*are the fathers of mankind*'.[12]

As we shall discover, for the Maya, the future was believed to be a repetition and variation of what had happened in the past, especially during specific periods of time such as the 20-year *katun* (*see* Appendix 4). Thus, prophecy and history were strangely mingled and, in this sense, prophecies are history repeating itself, since knowing the past meant knowing the cyclical influences that create both the present and the future. While the Mayan prophecies stand alone, they contribute to a tradition that was already both rich and ancient. Old Testament prophecies drew their authority from the integrity of the prophet, the authority of God, and the nature of the relationship between them. It seems that the closer, or more spiritual the relationship, the more authoritative and incisive is the prophecy. In its highest form, it becomes what has been termed 'ecstatic prophecy', a transmission that virtually overcomes the prophet/god duality. What we are considering is not simply a matter of concepts communicated by language, but an exchange, or a sharing of a unique kind of experience. The priest will have actual experience, at the highest spiritual level, of what he is required to communicate, in much the same way as he will have a perception of recurrences in the cyclic concept of time. These experiences are shamanistic and very persuasive.

Who were the prophets? They were called 'Chilam' or 'Chilan', a title, like the term 'priest', to which was added the epithet 'Balam', meaning jaguar. The jaguar figures considerably in Mayan mythology. It is said to be able to cross between worlds at a spiritual level, as it does between day and night which, for the Maya, represent different, but complementary, modes of being. The earth and everything that lives is associated with the day; the world of the spirit and the ancestors is associated with the night. Thus, Balam was a name assumed by the king, the ruling classes and an elite priesthood. 'Chilam', together with the name of the town of residence, gave the identifying title to the codices, for example, 'The Book of Chilam Balam' *of Chumayel.* Other surviving codices carry the names of places where their author, the Chilam, lived (*see* map page xi).

> There were several books of Chilam Balam; each community had its own book of the Chilam Balam [the Jaguar Priest]. Each community's Chilam Balam was written and maintained by its leader, usually a sage or priest, who wrote the name of the community in the Chilam for identification purposes. Thus, we have the Chilam Balam of Chumayel. Other than that of Chumayel, Mani, Tizimin, Kaua, Ixil and Tusik, no others seem to have survived the conquest intact; the other books of Chilam Balam (I was told that there were 13 in all) were destroyed by the Jesuits under edict of the Papal Bulls from Rome.[13]

The priests were thought to be directly descended from the original priesthood established by Quetzalcoatl, and the title 'Chilam' was used to indicate both their high rank and the special knowledge that merited their being priests with shamanic gifts. As such, they had a considerable agenda [14] which included such duties as, impersonating and invoking the deity, the drawing of the pebbles of the days and regulating the calendar, reading the weather and other omens from the clouds, studying the night sky and interpreting the appearance of the celestial bodies, determining the lucky and unlucky days for various mundane activities by the casting of lots, performing rituals, announcing the times for various agriculture and other activities to insure adequate rainfall, reading from the sacred scriptures the prophetic character of the *katun*, designing and supervising the carving of steles, the manufacture of wood and clay idols, the building of temples, and constructing tables of eclipses and heliacal risings of the planets such as are found in the Dresden Codex.

The central and most significant role of this 'special branch' of the priesthood was that of prophecy. One of the codices describes how the Chilam Balam of Tizimin, gave his prophecy, and the method is probably typical:

> He went into a room in his home and lay down,
> passing into a trance-like state. The
> communicating god or spirit, sat on the ridge of
> the house and spoke to the unconscious Chilan.
> When it was finished, other priests gathered in
> what may have been the reception hall of the
> house, and they listened, as the receiving prophet
> told them his message. They kept their faces
> bowed to the floor.[15]

The Mayan Prophecies fall, broadly, into five categories, day prophecies, year prophecies, *katun* prophecies, the prophecies of Pacal Votan (*see* Prophecy 5), and prophecies that speak of the return of the supreme being, Quetzalcoatl or Kukulcan (*see* Prophecy 4).

The day prophecies are prognostic, and are the business of the *ah-kinyah*, the diviner, and not the Chilam. Each of the 260 days of the Tzolk'in, or Tonalamatl (Appendix 2) is marked as either lucky or unlucky. The prognoses will indicate if the day is auspicious for sowing crops, trade, pursuing professional occupations etc.

The year prophecies are genuine and relate to the 20-year period of a specific *katun*, Katun 4 Ahau. There are two versions of these prophecies, one found in the Tizimin, the other in the Mani codex. In the latter, the title given to the prophecy is *'Cuceb'* - squirrel, though the significance of the name is not really understood. The nature of the pre-dictions is reminiscent of those of the minor Hebrew prophets, in that they warn of drought, famine, pestilence, war, political unrest, the destruction of towns, the captivity of the people. Many of the predictions are symbolized by the names of the deities who brought them to the Chilam and to religious ceremonies. These references come solely from a native source and are therefore of particular importance because much of our knowledge of Mayan religion comes from Spanish and, thus, prejudiced sources.

The *katun* prophecies were written in European script in the Books of Chilam Balam. That they are close to the hieroglyphic originals is confirmed by the accounts given by Father Avendano, who was one of the original, invading scholar missionaries. He was particularly interested in the 20-year *katun* prophecies, and drew his information from an original hieroglyphic codex of the Itza. In his account, Avendano recorded:

> I told them that I wished to speak to them of the old manner of reckoning which they use, both of days, months and years and of the ages, and to find out what age the present one might be (since for them one age consists only of twenty years) and what prophecy there was about the said year and age; for it is all recorded in certain books of a quarter of a yard high and about five fingers broad, made of the bark of trees, folded from one side to the other like screens; each leaf of the thickness of a Mexican Real [former coin] of eight. These are painted on both sides with a variety of figures and characters (of the same kind as the Mexican Indians also used in their old times), which shows not only the count of the said days, months and years, but also the ages and prophecies which their idols and images

announced to them, or, to speak more accurately, the devil by means of the worship which they pay to him in the form of some stones. These ages are thirteen in number; each age has its separate idol and its priest, with a separate prophecy of its events. These thirteen ages are divided into thirteen parts, which divide this kingdom of Yucatan and each age, with its idol, priest and prophecy, rules in one of these thirteen parts of this land, according as they have divided it ...[16]

From the very few documents that survived, we know that the 'cultural holocaust' perpetrated by the Spanish missionaries caused the Maya profound grief which the Chilam Balam of Tizimin noted: '*Should we not lament in our suffering, grieving for the loss of our maize and the destruction of our teachings concerning the universe of the earth and the universe of the heavens?*'[17] Only six named prophets emerge from the surviving accounts; Ah Xupan Nauat, Ah Kauil Chel, Napuctun, Natzin Yabun Chan, Nahau Pech, and the Chilam Balam referred to above. Other than this, we are left with only four codices written in Mayan hieroglyphics: the Paris Codex (found in a Paris library 1859), the Dresden Codex, which came to light in 1939, the Madrid Codex and the Grolier Codex. Apart from these there is a considerable record left in inscriptions carved on monuments, pyramids and steles, and painted on pottery.[18]

The rich and complex civilization of the Maya has left a lasting legacy. Its survival is due entirely to its extraordinary energy, itself, the life-current from which Mayan religion and culture drew. The Mayan vision, and its prophetic insights are uncannily relevant to our world. They offer a new view of the problems of pluralism, consumerism and materialism; they point to new solutions for the fracturing of society both nationally and internationally, and they speak directly to the ecological crisis facing our planet.

**Note** This introduction provides a brief account of the background necessary for placing the prophecies in their cultural and religious context. For well researched accounts of Mayan history, religion and culture, there is a very extensive literature available. Some of the most informative books are listed in the Further Reading chapter.

# THE
# PROPHECIES

*For the Maya, the relationship between cyclical
time, its units and the supernatural, readily
added the quality of divination to their
understanding of time. In a sense then, the
Maya inhabited an ongoing and continuous
world of prophecy. Thus the Maya prophecy is
far from a unique occurrence; it was a natural
part of everyday Maya life.*

R Bonewitz

*The Mayan prophecies exist because the Mayas
knew the cosmic time.*

Hunbatz Men

*Our psyche is set up in accord with the structure
of the universe, and what happens in the
macrocosm likewise happens in the infinitesimal
and most subjective reaches of the psyche.*

C G Jung

- I -

# PROPHECIES OF THE COMING OF FOREIGNERS & A NEW RELIGION

*Ahau is the beginning of the count, because this was the katun when the foreigners arrived. They came from the east when they arrived. Then Christianity also began. ... The katun is established at Ichcaanzihoo.*

Chilam Balam of Chumayel [19]

*Finally there came the great, the excessive sorrow of the sons of our wretchedness, when the foreigners descended from the sea. ... In 8 Ahau, the pueblo of Mayapan was abandoned on account of the mountains of foreigners.*

Chilam Balam of Tizimin [20]

The prophecy speaks of the catastrophic coming of foreigners who would bring a new religion. The foundation of Mayan prophecy is their cyclic concepts of time and history. Knowing what had occurred in a previous period enabled the prophets to indicate what was likely to recur. Thus, it is probable they knew their own civilization would disintegrate and then recover, only to succumb to the Spanish conquest. Why the decline of their civilization was not anticipated in the prophecies, remains a mystery.

## COMMENTARY

The one event in their own history for which the Maya offered no prophecy, was the decline and sudden disappearance of their civilization. Why this was so continues to be something of a mystery, but possible answers shed light on the character of the prophetic culture itself. During the 9th century CE, some kind of radical natural change brought the Mayan 'Classical' period to an end, an event marked by the sudden abandonment of their city states in Guatemala and the Yucatan lowlands. As a result of this seemingly unforeseen decline there was a gradual reduction of commemorative inscriptions. The evidence indicates that after certain dates no further stelae were raised and inscribed with the importantly celebrated *katun*-ending dates. During the period of the collapse of their civilization, only three sites recorded the *katun*-ending date of 889 CE (in Mayan numerology, 10.3.0.0.0 – *see* Appendix 4), and that the final Long Count date to be recorded was the *katun*-ending date 20 years later in 909 CE, (10.4.0.0.0) which was cut into a piece of jade.[21] Within a century, however, there was a remarkable renaissance of Mayan culture and civilization centred around magnificent ceremonial sites such as Chichén Itza, in northern Yucatan. This round of decline and regeneration is an example of how their own recurring history reflected their cyclic concept of time.

Many theories have been offered as to why Mayan civilization faded so quickly; these include warfare with another nation, a rebellion of the peasantry against the ruling priestly class, disease, soil erosion due to forest clearing, the subsequent failure of agriculture to support an increased population, a massive natural disaster such as flood, earthquake or comet impact, or a combination of these. No archaeological evidence has been found that adequately supports such theories. Whatever the causes, the greater problem remains – why, in a culture founded on prophecy, was the event not predicted? The lack of prophecy does not necessarily mean the Maya were in ignorance of what might happen. Their veiled origins are to be traced to previous civilizations each of which fell into decay, such as the Olmec and the Zapotec. Because of their cyclic concept of time, the Maya understood that history was also cyclic and that events of the past were likely, at least in general terms, to recur. Based on the precedents of Olmec and Zapotec decline, they would have had some presentiment of their own civilization's mortality, just as they would of its post-Classical resurgence, which in turn was overthrown by the Spanish conquest. This latter misfortune was, as we shall see, clearly prophesied.

The decline of Mayan society is identified with specific 20-year periods called *katuns* (Appendix 4). Each *katun* was believed to have certain characteristics and of those broadly covering the period in the 9th century when Mayan culture began to fall apart, the 3rd *katun*, Katun 7 Ahau, is associated with '*Carnal sin. Roguish rulers*' and the 4th *katun*, Katun 5 Ahau as, '*Harsh is his face, harsh his feelings*'.[22] Unsurprisingly, the prophecies based on the character of these *katuns* are decidedly unfavourable, and speak of radical change. That this was clearly indicated, was probably enough to prepare the Maya, enabling them to respond, or adapt, to whatever Earth-changing crisis occurred. As we shall see, the concept of change becomes one of central importance for the prophecies pointing to 2012.

While the prophecies of the decline of Mayan civilization

were not given, the prophecies of conquest were clearly pointed. Probably the best known are the *katun* prophecies from the books of Chilam Balam, telling of the coming of strangers, who turned out to be the Spanish; equally clear, are prophecies of the conquerors bringing a new religion. These prophecies were thought to have been given a considerable time before the events occurred. The fullest surviving account is that of a prophet living around the year 1500 CE, thus, just before the Conquest. He was known as the Cabalchen, the singer of Mani. His prophecy for the 20-year period, Katun 13 Ahau, ending about 1539, is, '*Behold, within seven score years Christianity will be introduced amid the clamour of the rulers – those who violently seize land during the katun*'.[23] A much earlier, 11th-century prophet Ah Xupan Naut predicted the coming of white men specifically during the 8th year of Katun 13 Ahau, which, starting in 1519, would give the year 1527. Montejo landed on the east coast of the Yucatan just a year later. This is an astoundingly accurate prophecy to be carried over so long a period as 500 years, and its language is a clear example of how the original prophecies were rewritten by the Christian conquerors so as to align them with actual events for which they, themselves, were responsible. The 16th-century prophet, the Chilam Balam of Tizimin and Mani, unambiguously predicted:

Then shall be known the time of the white men,
the bearded ones, just as the priest Chilam
declared the time of the arrival of their elder
brothers, just as the host of Itza arrived among
them. You shall intermarry with them, you shall
dress in their garments, you shall put on their
hats, you shall speak their language.[24]

There is no doubt, however, that the prophet's intended message was the return of Quetzalcoatl (*see* Prophecy 4). However, on this occasion, it was not the mystic god who arrived, but the more mundane Cortez who made landfall in Mexico in 1519, precisely the year Katun 13 Ahau started. The Chilam's prophecy reads:

There is the sign of Hunab K'u [the one true God]
on high. The raised wooden standard shall come.
It shall be displayed to the world, that the world
might be enlightened, Lord. There has been the
beginning of strife, there has been a beginning of
rivalry, when the priestly men shall come to bring
the sign in time to come. ... Receive your guests,
the bearded men, the men of the east, the bearers
of the sign of God, Lord. Good indeed is the word
of God that comes to us. The day of our
regeneration comes.[25]

The 'wooden standard' of the prophecy was a figure of the Cross, 'the sign' a reference to it being a symbol of the one true God. As the prophecy continues there are clear indications of the influence of Spanish missionaries on the Mayan writers who compiled the books, and who had succumbed to some form of Christianity. Somewhat inevitably, the prophecies are interpreted here as a vindication of the new religion. If the Maya were made to believe that the coming of Christianity was part of traditional prophecy, conversion would follow more easily. It would have made a huge impression on them that Cortez turned up in 1519, the actual year prophesied for the Quetzalcoatl return. Furthermore, it would not have been difficult for Catholic missionaries to exploit this seemingly Messianic hope and align it with that of Christ's Second Coming, thus Christianizing Mayan eschatology.

The four following prophecies relate to other specific events in Mayan history.

### SUMMARY

The extent to which the Maya were aware of the coming decline of their Classical civilization is uncertain, but the destruction, at a later date, of their resurgent culture by the Spanish is among the clearest of their prophecies. That being so, the general weight of the prophecy was to give early indication of radical and challenging change, and a warning to prepare for it. Radical change is a theme that runs through all the prophecies pointing us to the climax of 2012. The principle is also established that the prophecies were bound up with the Maya's sense of time recurring in cycles, and with specific periods of time having particular characteristics that determined the nature of the events that would recur.

# THE PROPHECY OF THE EMERGENCE OF CONTEMPORARY MAYAN MASTERS & TEACHERS

*Katun 7 Ahau is the third katun. Yaxal Chac is the face of the katun in the heavens, to its rulers, to its wise man ... There is no great teaching. Heaven and Earth are truly lost to them; ... Then the head-chiefs of the towns, the rulers of the towns, the prophets of the towns, the priests of the Maya men are hanged. Understanding is lost; wisdom is lost.*

**Chilam Balam of Chumayel** [26]

*These Masters will come from many places. They will be of many colours. Some will speak of things difficult to understand. Others will be aged. Some less so. Some will dance while others will remain silent as rocks. Their eyes will communicate the initiatic message, which is to continue through the cycles of the next millennium.*

Hunbatz Men [27]

### THE MESSAGE

The prophets predicted a time when their ancient, hidden knowledge would be recovered and given to the world by a future generation of elders and time keepers. Despite the persistent execution of their prophets and teachers by the Spanish colonizers, and the destruction of all but a few of their sacred codices, the Maya were able to preserve their traditional wisdom literature. The prophecy speaks of our urgent need of teachers who, by sharing this recovered wisdom, will lead us back to the basic, but ominously neglected sources of self-fulfilment, and of life itself.

## COMMENTARY

Over recent years the teachings and writings of contemporary Mayan elders and time keepers have attracted increasing interest in the West. This is undoubtedly due to the ancient prophecies being tied to the end date of their Long Count Calendar, the winter equinox of the 21 December, 2012. The presence of these Masters during the last *katun* of the final *baktun* of this age, was prophesied and their emergence as custodians of ancient Mayan wisdom is a fulfilment of that prophecy. Hunbatz Men (quoted above) is a modern Mayan *hau-k-in*, or teacher, and is himself believed to be a fulfilment of the prophecy of the reincarnation of the earlier Masters and of their return to the sacred sites of the Maya (*see* Prophecy 3). Prophecies given to the Mayan Itzas during the 9th and 10th centuries CE, that is, sometime between the sudden demise of their civilization and its resurgence in northern Yucatan, told of the future return of the initiates to the sacred land of the Maya. They are destined to continue the work of Hunab K'u, the Great Spirit or originator of 'Measure and Movement' (*see* Introduction). The mandate given to the new generation of teachers was in the form of prophecy, the time will come *'to join together and work in harmony to heal the past and rehabilitate the planet and establish an era of alignment and peace'.*[28]

The contemporary Mayan astrologer and spiritual guide, Aluna Joy Yaxk'in', describes how in 1475, shortly before the first arrival of Columbus, an assembly of the Supreme Council of Maya Priests gathered to prepare for a period of darkness that was about to engulf the Maya, prophesied to begin with the invasion of the Spanish. It was this Council that decided, *'to keep this cosmic wisdom secret'*. It was further prophesied that two calendar cycles (two cycles of 260 years, thus, 520 years) would elapse before their ancient wisdom emerged, once more, into the light. At the spring equinox of 1995, 520 years on from the given prophecy, Hunbatz Men conducted a solar initiation at one of the most important of the ancient ceremonial sites, Chichen Itza. This event was regarded as the first step of the fulfilment of the prophecy that the original, hidden wisdom of the Maya would be made known through reincarnated Masters and, *'that initiates shall return to the sacred land of the Mayas, ... to communicate their secrets'*.[29] For the Maya, 1995 was, as Roys put it, the beginning of the transition from *'an age of belief, to an age of knowledge'* (*see* Prophecies 11 and 13). Hunbatz Men's solar initiation

> ... offered a genuine spiritual experience for the tens of thousands who attended, most of whom were Mayan. The day was filled with wonder. Lamas from Tibet and leaders of the Supreme Mayan Council bestowed blessings upon attendees.[30]

Hunbatz Men's solar initiation at Chichen Itza in 1995 was, therefore, a fulfilment in part, of the prophecies that speak of the re-emergence of teachers and Masters, and the reclamation of the sacred sites (*see* Prophecy 3). Hunab K'u, the name for the Mayan concept of an absolute god, intelligence or principle, is the focus of solar initiation the consequences of which give energy to other prophecies such as those of the unity of humanity, a new 'Enlightenment', and awakened cosmic consciousness (*see* Prophecies 11, 12 and 13).

The events of 1994–95 brought to an end the prophesied 'Age of Darkness' during which the teachings were 'hidden'. These events also provide a back-baring for what happened to the Maya during the 9th and 10th centuries which saw the sudden and enigmatic decline of their southern civilization, its later, northern restoration, and the 16th-century conquest of the Maya and their conversion to Christianity. The fate of an entire and sophisticated civilization describes cycles of resurgence and decline, and the same pattern recurred in the final decade of the 20th century when, after 500 years of 'darkness', the Maya gathered together once more to carry their wisdom to the world. This prophecy, that the Mayan culture would rise from the jungle ruins again, as it had in the 10th century, is confirmed by Hunbatz Men:

> The Mayan prophecies are being fulfilled. Some
> are being fulfilled even now. Some will be fulfilled
> on the morrow. The Mayan prophecies exist
> because the Mayas knew the cosmic time. They
> knew that in certain times it would be necessary to
> keep this cosmic wisdom secret. This was the
> purpose of the prophecy so that they might be
> able to communicate their secrets to the initiates
> of the future.[31]

It can be argued that every definitive passage in the history
of the world's religious evolution has been associated with
a teacher, or teachers, such as the early Vedic *rishis*, Buddha,
Moses, Jesus, Zoroaster, Mohammed, Baha'ullah etc. The
clear implication of the prophecy is that advanced teachers
of all religions will join together in carrying to the world
the urgent message of its need of spiritual rejuvenation.

### SUMMARY

The core subject of the prophecy is the return of the
'initiates of the future' to the sacred land of the Maya. The
responsibility of this new generation of Masters is to point
the way that will enable people to experience '*cosmic wisdom*'
(*see* Prophecy 11) and to continue the work of the 'Great
Spirit'. There is, however, one crucial new element in the
fulfilment of this prophecy. The teachers will not be drawn

exclusively from the Maya. Initiates will be taken from a cross-section of people of all cultures and religions, from both the young and the old regardless of sex, race or class. Their main concern will be to redress the problems caused by the failure of our society to meet its educational ideals and responsibilities, and to correct the extent to which the negative influences of a materialistic education, technology, and the overuse of the planet's natural resources, have restricted our spiritual development.

# THE PROPHECY OF THE RETURN TO THE MAYAN CEREMONIAL SITES

*When the thirteenth tun arrives on his* [the Year-bearer's] *day and 13 Muluc falls on the first day of Pop, on the day 1 Oc there will be majesty, when Pop shall descend, when Zam shall descend in Tun 13. At the ceremonies there will be overwhelming grandeur, the impressive majesty of the heavens.*

The Book of Chilam Balam of Tizimin [32]

*The Mayan ceremonial centres begin to emanate the light of the new millennium which is much needed today. Many Mayan cosmic ceremonial centres begin to beckon with their solar reflection the many initiates who will come to continue the work of the Great Spirit.*

Hunbatz Men [33]

### THE MESSAGE

It is prophesied that the elders and teachers will return to the ancient Mayan sites mysteriously abandoned in the 9th century. This is a call to recognize and return to all the places that are known to be sacred, whether they be hills, mountains, groves, rivers, lakes or places of worship that focus the collective spiritual energy of all religions.

COMMENTARY

> There exist four Mayan ceremonial centres of
> importance which energy must be activated so that
> their energy of light may serve to illuminate the
> steps humanity must take in this new
> millennium.[34]

The extensive and awe-inspiring Mayan ceremonial sites, first came to the attention of the West in 1773 with the discovery of its most celebrated city, Palenque. Since then, exploration and archaeology have steadily disclosed many more. It is only in the second half of the 20th century that we have been able to decipher the hieroglyphic inscriptions carved over the walls of many of the temples, and on the surfaces of steles and other monuments. These sites hold a huge amount of hieroglyphic information, and their excavation and the breaking of the Mayan code has made them an 'open book'. Despite the huge, worldwide interest this has generated, and the inevitable surge in tourism to the Yucatan and Guatemala, the fulfilment of the prophecy of the elders' return to the sites is regarded has having begun only in 1995, when Hunbatz Men led the solar initiation at Chichen Itza. It followed, that for the new generation of Mayan masters and initiates, the sites lost to the jungle should not only be recovered and restored, but reused as the ceremonial centres they originally were. A more literal fulfilment of the prophecy of reclaiming the sites, cannot be imagined.

Among the significant centres that have been recovered are: Ek Balam, Oxkintok, Mayapan, Palenque, Chichen Itza, and Tikal; these were sacred to the Maya and remain so. What has been recovered at the ceremonial sites is 'the sacred energy of the Masters', who learned of the new form of initiation. Perhaps, inevitably, the millennium of the Gregorian calendar in 2000 CE also drew the masters and elders back to these sites. Hunbatz Men has explained that, *'in many Mayan ceremonial centres Solar Priests* [will] *begin to walk among the multitude of tourists. They will be touched by the Solar Priests to be initiated with cosmic wisdom'.*[35] Prior to the millennium, it was the significance given in the Mayan calendar to the spring equinox of 21 March 1995, that was of special importance in marking the first phase in the fulfilment of this prophecy.

As with other aspects of the prophecies touching on the Maya's own history and culture, their message is not confined to the Maya or to their tradition of wisdom. The prophecies speak of our need to recognize the spiritual energy focused in the sacred sites of all religions, for example, the Sikh Golden Temple in Amritsar, the Temple Mount and Wailing Wall in Jerusalem, the Ka'aba in Mecca, Stonehenge in Wiltshire, St Peter's in Rome, and Bodhgaya, the place of the Buddha's enlightenment. For various and obvious reasons, such sites are frequently in the news, their true significance obscured by the politics of violence and prejudice. Innumerable natural sacred sites exist that have not been touched by the main religious traditions, and many of these places are vibrant with spiritual energy. Aboriginal and tribal religions have retained their sense of numinal awe for mountains, rivers, groves, song lines, ley lines and caves. This prophecy requires us to consider, not just the formally or traditionally sacred sites that have been constructed, but to recover our sense of the sacredness of nature, everywhere evident, but concentrated in specific locations.

### SUMMARY

Western culture's sensitivity to 'place' has been numbed by fundamentalism and the politics of institutional religion and sectarianism. We no longer sense the numinous power and holiness of the sacred sites. In this respect, India is both an exception and an example:

> India is a vast network of sacred places. The entire country is a sacred land. The sacredness of the land of India is what, still today, gives a sense of unity to this country of so many religions, cultures, races and factions.[36]

Wherever we live, and whatever path we follow, the prophecy calls us to recover our sensitivity to places charged with spiritual energy and knowledge. It is a further reminder that we should regain a closer relationship with nature (*see* Prophecy 19).

- 4 -

# THE PROPHECY OF THE RETURN OF A SUPREME BEING

*Would that he might return from the west, uniting us in commiseration over our present unhappy plight! This is the fulfilment of the prophecies of Katun 5 Ahau. ... God grant that there may come a Deliverer from our afflictions, who will answer our prayers in Katun 1 Ahau!*

**Chilam Balam of Tizimin** [37]

## THE MESSAGE

The prophecy of the return of a Supreme Teacher or Being, speaks of Quetzalcoatl, known to the Maya as, Kukulcan. However, there is a growing belief that this will not take the form of an actual return or reincarnation, but of people themselves taking on the character and attributes of the Supreme Being through their own spiritual evolution, to the point of overcoming the duality of the subject-object relationship. It is a prophecy that resonates with all religions.

❖

## COMMENTARY

Much lies behind this prophecy, and to understand its significance we need to trace in a little background.

Mayan mythology has, to a great extent, pivoted around Quetzalcoatl, the plumed or feathered serpent, one of the principal gods of Mesoamerican religion, whom the Maya called, Kukulcan. His cult and its influence was not confined to the Toltec-Maya, and his emblem, the feathered serpent, is found throughout Mexico. Much of Mesoamerican religion, and one of the principal Mayan prophecies, was focused on the belief that Kukulcan would return. This belief was so deeply embedded, that in November 1519, Montezuma II, ruler of the Aztecs, virtually surrendered to Cortez believing him to be either an emissary of Quetzalcoatl or the god himself, newly reincarnated. He greeted Cortez with the words, '*My royal ancestors have said that you would come to visit your city and that you would sit upon your mat and chair when you returned*'.[38] The *katun* that most clearly prophesied the return of Quetzalcoatl is Katun 4 Ahau:

> The *katun* is established at Chichen Itza. The settlement of the Itza shall take place [there]. The quetzal shall come, the green bird shall come. Ah Kantenal shall come. Blood-vomit shall come. Kukulcan shall come with them for the second time.[39]

'Blood-vomit' is thought to be yellow fever, referring either to a an actual plague, or used as a metaphor for the Spanish invasion. The point made, is that Kukulcan will return at the time of the people's greatest need. Aluna Joy Yaxk'in suggests that, '*Kukulkan (the Feathered Serpent God, also known as Quetzalcoatl) is to the New World what Christ is to Europe: the centre of a religious cosmology and the pre-eminent symbol of the civilized nations of Mesoamerica*'.[40]

It is hardly surprising that Spanish missionaries, like the 17th-century Father Avendano, rationalized the prophecy of the coming of Kukulcan as the Spanish conquest and the Maya's conversion to Christianity. However, behind the missionary's Christianization of the prophecies lies a genuine and very ancient native tradition. The American anthropologist and linguist Alfred Tozzer explained that, *'these prophecies were doubtless adapted by the Spanish to proselytizing purposes but they seem fundamentally to have been native accounts of the return of Kukulcan, one of the culture heroes of the Maya, and corresponding to the Quetzalcoatl of the Mexicans'.*[41] It is, therefore, beyond question, that the prophecies of the Jaguar Priests are imbedded in ancient tradition, and predate Christian influence.

Quetzalcoatl is frequently represented as a feathered or plumed serpent, and because of this serpent symbolism, the prophecies of the return of Quetzalcoatl/Kukulcan have important associations with the esoteric parallel of Hinduism's secret knowledge of *k'ulthanlilni* (kundalini) and the seven chakras, the body's centres of energy. Although there is a tradition that before the Christian era Mayan elders and priests travelled to India taking their knowledge with them, the influence remains conjectural. Even so, it is remarkable that the Maya taught about the seven power centres of the human body by which means the energy of the cosmos was assimilated and expressed. It may well be a striking example of parallel development. In Hindu teaching, kundalini represents a serpent-like potential curled at the base of the spine. Specific techniques of yoga and meditation can 'awaken' this serpent whose energy rises through the seven chakras; training in this technique under the necessary guidance of a guru or teacher is one of the many 'paths' to liberation. In Mayan mythology, the source of this energy lies in the Earth from where it begins to move; first, to the base of the spine, then through each of the seven chakras. This vital link between the Earth and the body is one of the central themes of the prophecies that speak of the urgent need of humanity to recover its innate relationship with Nature (*see* Prophecies 12, 14 and 19).

This prophecy of the return of Quetzalcoatl has a dimension that lies beyond the myth; it speaks of a resurgence of the kind of energy used in kundalini meditation that will take many creative forms. Thus 'return' can be read as a 'resurgence' of a fire-like spread of energy and the transformation of consciousness that leads, in turn, to the individual transcending an earthbound, materialistic way of life. In Mayan mythology it is the cycles of Venus (*see* Prophecy 9) that signal the return of Kukulcan/ Quetzalcoatl, and the consequent expanding or unfolding of human consciousness. According to the prophecy, Kukulcan promised he would return after '*five full cycles of the dawn star*', that is, Venus as the Morning Star. It is to be noted that the galactic synchronization (*see* Prophecy 6) of December 2012 will be preceded by a transit of Venus on 6 June (*see* Prophecy 9).

Thus far, we have a prophecy that speaks of the return of

a god which, understood literally or otherwise, will liberate earthbound energies, and revitalize our consciousness and the life of the spirit. Beyond this, the prophecy carries a message of broader significance pointing to a Supreme Being, that is, to the Mayan monotheism of the one true god, Hunab K'u.

In Mayan tradition, many of the prophecies of the return of Kukulcan are found in the Books of Chilam Balam, for example, in that of Tizimin. Here, various names for the god are used, but it is already clear that the prophet's intention was to establish the *one god* represented by the different names. In the Book of Chilam Balam of Chumayel, the section, 'Prophecies of a New Religion' are known to be the special prophecies of the return of Kukulcan or Quetzalcoatl. Like all mythologies, those of the Maya changed and developed progressively. In this case, the accounts of Quetzalcoatl and Kukulcan tell of how these once separately conceived deities, have gradually become one, regardless of the names used. A useful illustration is to be found in the accounts of the Old Testament of how the names for God – 'Elohim', 'Adonai', 'Yahweh' – each one an expression of the radical monotheism characteristic of Judaism, came to represent the one God. It can be argued that after the sudden decline of the Mayan 'Classical' period, one of the inspirations behind the resurgence of their culture was this movement towards monotheism, when the writings begin to show the elision of Quetzalcoatl and Kukulkan, and the emerging conception of Hunab K'u as the one god. The transition from decline to resurgence, thus traces the path the Maya took towards a genuine spiritual sophistication. What this element of the prophecy points to is yet another theme passing through the prophecies, namely, as we approach 2012, one of the conditions that must be met if we are to solve the problems of our civilization and the planet Earth, is the extent to which we can realize the unity of the human race *as a figure* of the unity of God (*see* Prophecy 11).

Most of the major world religions hold to an expectation of the coming of a Supreme Being, Teacher or Saviour. Jews focus on the Messianic hope, Christians on the Second Coming of Christ, Islam on the return of Jesus the prophet and the Mahdi. Hinduism holds to traditions such as that of Kalki, Buddhism to a concept of the Maitreya, the 'loving one', the fifth and last of the five earthly Buddhas. Robert Boissière's> account of the belief in an imminent return of a type of teacher or saviour among native and aboriginal people, suggests that their beliefs are similar to the Christian expectation of the 'Second Coming' of Jesus. Each of these traditions, preserving as they do the myth of a returning saviour or leader, also have in common the assurance that the return will be linked to a time when both humanity and the Earth are at risk.

## SUMMARY

Contemporary Mayan elders have a somewhat different take on what the return of Kukulcan actually means; they confirm that a broader, rather than a literal, interpretation does greater justice to the message. Thus, the prophecy is seen not so much as a physical return of an ancient god, but that through the:

> initiation of cosmic wisdom people can attain the same, high spiritual state, so as to 'become' Kukulcan. ... From this moment on, I would like you to realize that we are all Quetzalcoatl or Kukulcan. We need only to develop our faculties of consciousness to fully realize that status.[42]

The ideal is consistent with other religions that seek union with a divine, or ultimate being.

- 5 -

# THE PROPHECIES
# OF PACAL VOTAN

*As the special witness of time, I, Pacal Votan,
know the perfect count of days. I bow in the
temple of the tower and the rock, the sanctuary
of Bolon Ik. In my body, formed of the ultimate
perfection of God's power of all movement and
measure (Hunab K'u), is the recollection that
is prophecy.*

**Pacal Votan** [43]

One of the meanings of the name 'Pacal Votan' is 'Closer of the Cycle', that is closer of the Great Cycle of time that concludes with the winter solstice 21 December, 2012. Thus, the prophecies of this 7th-century Mayan prophet-king are of particular significance.

## COMMENTARY

The prophecies of the Mayan king, Pacal Votan (603–683 CE) stand alone, and in order to appreciate their relevance and strength, his background and context need to be sketched in.

Pacal Votan was only 12 when he came to the throne in July 615 CE, and from his base at Nah Chan Palenque, the present-day Chiapas, he ruled the Mayan empire for 52 years. He was responsible for a programme of building that included some the finest examples of Mayan art and architecture, but he is renowned also for the inscriptions carved on to these monuments recording precise astronomical and astrological information. Because of these, he is known as the 'Magician of Time', or 'Time's Special Witness', communicating through a mathematical system using numbers that transcend conventional forms of language. His central principle was: '*All is number. God is number. God is in all.*' As already noted, in Yucatec Mayan the supreme being is called 'Hunab K'u', which can mean the 'Giver of Movement and Measure', the 'Source', or the 'Galactic Centre'. Thus Pacal Votan can be thought of as an 'avatar' of Hunab K'u, or to have been inspired by him.

Interred in his famous tomb, the Temple of Inscriptions at Palenque, Pacal was worshipped as a god. When Ruz discovered the tomb in 1952, the excavations disclosed a stone tube running from the chamber enclosing the sar-cophagus, to the temple floor above. The tube is known to archaeologists as a 'psychoduct' or Telektonon.

> The Kings of Palenque were practical men as well
> as people of faith. To help their ancestors ascend
> to the world of humankind, they created a physical
> path for the Vision Serpent to follow when a dead
> king wished to speak to his descendents.[44]

It is thought that Pacal Votan's prophecies were communi-cated in this way. '*This was not, it would seem, a means of ventilation, more a kind of spiritual wiring.*' [45] The prophecies were '*mythically emanated*' to be received by the priests who came to consult Pacal Votan and seek his advice. The system thus worked in much the same way as the classical oracle. The name 'Pacal' has various meanings, one of which is 'shield'. An alternative, referred to above, is 'Closer of the Cycle', thus, it can be said that his prophecies speak of the closing of this World Age cycle on 21 December 2012. Hunbatz Men tells us the priests believed that *the spirit of Pacal Votan came from the stars and that he brought the wisdom of the stars with him*.[46] This 'Wisdom' is believed to be the source of the Maya's astronomical and mathematical knowledge, and also of a more esoteric knowledge already referred to as the secrets of *k'ulthanlilni*, known in Eastern mysticism as kundalini (*see* Prophecy 4). The technique of kundalini meditation, probably practised by the prophetic Chilam, generated the energy that was expressed as prophecy. The priests, mathematicians and astronomers were given specific times when they could mount the steps of the pyramid to approach Pacal Votan, and it was in this way that those with responsibility could be given some form of spiritual guidance in order to direct the people towards the ideal life. The Telektonon or Colophon emanations of Pacal Votan consulted by Mayan notabilities, were a 'talking stone of prophecy'. Hunbatz Men likened Pacal Votan to the Sun, he:

> came to this world to illuminate his Mayan people.
> He came from the dimension where the
> enlightened teachers are waiting for the right
> moment to get reincarnated [*see* Prophecy 2]. It is

there where the Universal Creator chooses the teacher who will come to fulfil the mission of guiding his people towards the cosmic light of wisdom.[47]

One such reincarnated teacher is José Argüelles who, believing himself to be the heir of Pacal Votan and an instrument of his prophecy, calls himself Valum Votan. Argüelles[48] has transcribed the Telektonon prophecies to show they have the following two themes.

Firstly, as we have noted, Pacal Votan is the 'Closer of the Cycle', and his prophecies point to the end of the current World Age in 2012. The prophecies are not of a terminal catastrophe, but of an evolving Earth and of a spiritual evolution of the people who inhabit it. He anticipated the extreme materialism of our age, the damage that would be caused to the Earth's biosphere by uncontrolled technology, and the deep spiritual harm that would be inflicted by humanity's separation from Nature and natural laws. His prophecies warn us that, as the *katuns* roll by towards 2012, our estrangement from nature will become one of humanity's greatest problems. Conscious of the larger cycles of time encoded in the calendars, Pacal Votan:

knew that humanity as a species would become disconnected from the laws of the natural world and would fall ignorant of our sacred interdependence with nature. He also knew that modern humanity would be put to the test to see if we can regain our conscious connection to natural time as the universal frequency of synchronization, evolving beyond the constructs of man-made linear time.[48]

Secondly, as we approach 2012, we have to give heed to one of the dominant themes running through the prophecies, namely, their warning that our transition into the next age is going to be problematic. To ease that transition, we will have to make decisions that require radical change; one of these, Argüelles argues, is the need to move from a 12- to a 13-Moon calendar cycle (*see* Prophecy 20). The implementation of other important changes will be dependent on people with vision and revised values. Pacal Votan's prophecy confronts us with the challenge that we are those people (*see* Prophecy 21); the generations living through the final *katun* of this age are the generations that have inherited the responsibility for change.

Perhaps the most penetrating insight of Pacal Votan's prophecies is the reference to the 26,000-year cycle of precession as a measure of the evolutionary process (*see* Prophecies 6 and 18). The prophecy alerts us to the fact that human biology is constantly transforming, an insight confirmed by current research that shows our DNA is not a fixed genetic vehicle, but one constantly in a process of adaptation. The prophecy points to a wider agenda of evolution than is represented by standard human biology. It anticipates the evolution of what, until now, have been thought of as 'fringe' human faculties such as interpersonal and universal telepathy, and a transformation of consciousness (*see* Prophecy 13). However, 2012 is not seen as the date when all of this will suddenly come about, but as with all evolutionary development, as signifying a time when the process itself will take centre stage with a new, critical interest in the 'fringe' faculties suggested above.

## SUMMARY

Pacal Votan's epigram, '*All is number. God is number. God is in all*', links with the name for the Mayan Absolute, Hunab K'u, '*the Giver of Movement and Measure*'. The two concepts bind to suggest that mathematics, together with movement and measure, is the source of life. Balance, order and harmony combine to be the expression of both the spiritual and physical life of the cosmos. The prophecy calls us to use personal, collective and cosmic energy to transcend the materialism and techno-dominance of our age, to prepare for the problematic transition into the next World Age. In this process, humanity will experience the evolutionary development of new creative and communicative faculties.

# THE PROPHECY OF GALACTIC SYNCHRONIZATION

*Then comes another law also in 4 Khan, the time of movement and noise in the sky, movement and noise on Earth. The Sun and the Earth shall come together within the district, the naval of the katun.*

**Chilam Balam of Tizimin and Man** [49]

*All moons, all years, all days, all winds, reach their completion. Measured is the time in which we can know the benevolence of the Sun. Measured is the time in which the stars look down on us.*

**Popul Vuh** [50]

## THE MESSAGE

The prophecy concerns huge energies to be released as a result of a conjunction of planets that takes place every 26,000 years. The event, which will occur at the winter equinox, 21 December, 2012, is called 'galactic synchronization'. The Earth and the solar system will be in conjunction with the rest of the universe and the plane of our solar system will be exactly in line with the plane of our galaxy, the Milky Way. The prophecy tells us that this synchronization marks the end of our old World Age, and the birth of a new one.

## COMMENTARY

The broader context of this prophecy is the Mayan concept of time, and their understanding of the nature of its relationship with space. Their awareness of this relationship was carried to the point where it became the principal influence on their culture and way of life. In one sense, sky-watching was the heart of their religion, and the 'raising' of the sky the focal point of the Quiché Mayan account of Creation (*see* Introduction). The Maya's knowledge of astronomy was accumulated by recording data over many centuries, and despite the limitations of naked-eye observation of the night sky, the accuracy of the data was assured by their knowledge of mathematics. It was this combination of advanced mathematics and documented data that enabled the Maya to predict that, by completing a cycle of approximately 26,000 years, the planet Earth would be brought into universal synchronization in 2012 CE. It is the consequences and significance of galactic synchronization with which this prophecy is concerned.

Unsurprisingly, the prophecies associated with astronomy are the most fully researched. One reason for this is that while the meaning of the astronomical conjunctions at the time of the winter solstice of 2012 CE is a matter of interpretation, the astronomy itself can be verified. One of the universities responsible for researching the conjunction and alignments of planets in 2012 is the Fernbank Science Centre Planetarium of Emory University, Atlanta, Georgia. Their conclusions show that *'planets such as Mercury, Venus, Mars, Jupiter, Saturn, the Sun and new Moon will come into alignment with the Earth in a most unique conjunction or union'.* [51] The suggestion is that these bodies will be connected by an invisible gravitational line of energy; it is these energies and the way they will affect the Earth that lie at the heart of this prophecy.

To understand the theme of the prophecy more fully, account must be taken of what is called 'precession', since the convergence we are concerned with is a precessional alignment of the Sun and the Milky Way at the time of the 2012 winter solstice. It was the Maya's discovery of precession that provided the ground for their concept of 'Suns' or World Ages and also for the creation myth recorded in the *Popul Vuh*. Jenkins sums up the matter succinctly: *'the end date of the Long Count Calendar in 2012 pinpoints a rare alignment in a vast cycle of time called the precession of the equinoxes.'*[52]

We have noted that the cycle of time is 26,000 years. What, then, is precession? It is the consequence of the Earth spinning on its axis once every 24 hours as it orbits the Sun, and the fact that in so doing it also wobbles. Because of this combination of spin and wobble over a long period, the location of a constellation of stars, seen from a specific point on the Earth at a particular time, will alter. What this amounts to is that a slow variation will take place in the *direction* of the Earth's axis, thus constellations will be seen from a gradually changing point of view. It is this change that is known to astronomers as 'precession'. The Maya were able to work with vast periods of time and calculated that it would take a cycle of approximately 26,000 years for a constellation to reappear over the same observation point on Earth. Modern astronomy has confirmed this period as 25,800 years. At this point, it is useful to remind ourselves of the Mayan concept of the 'Five Suns', or solar periods.

We are currently moving towards the end of the Fifth Sun, its period marked by the beginning and end dates of the Long Count Calendar, that is, 13 August 3114 BCE, and 21 December 2012 CE, a period of 5,126 years. It is the longer, approximately, 26,000-year period of the *Five* Suns with which precession is concerned, the termination of which will return the galaxy to the conjunction observed at the beginning of the First Sun. The Maya thought of each Sun as a World Age, or 'creative cycle'. Contemporary Mayan timekeepers in Guatemala offer an alternative chronology, teaching that we are coming to the end of the fourth cycle, with the fifth starting 21 December 2012. Astronomically, the principle is the same, as is the implication of the prophecy, namely that our old world is passing away, and we are rapidly approaching the moment when a new world, or World Age, will be born. Joel Davis has explained that:

> We are 26,000 light years away from the Galactic Centre. Recalling that the full cycle of precession is 26,000 years, this means that the light, or 'energy' reaching us now from the Galactic Centre began its journey toward us during the last era in which the December solstice Sun conjuncted the Galactic Centre – in 24000 BCE. We can only wonder what this strange coincidence of numbers might mean. Are we currently experiencing some kind of time

resonance with the Earth of 24000 BCE. Are we
receiving archaic messages through the 2012 time-
doorway knowledge to help us evolve? What is it
about the Galactic Centre that might make this
possible? [53]

What will actually happen is that at sunrise on 21 December
2012, the Sun forms a conjunction with the galactic centre
of the Milky Way and the plane of the Sun's path, or ecliptic
which crosses the Milky Way at the constellation of Scorpio
(*see* Prophecy 7). Because of the precision of the equinoxes
the winter solstice sunrise has been moving towards that
point on the Milky Way known as the 'galactic centre'. Thus,
the planet Earth and the solar system will come into galactic
conjunction with the rest of the universe.

It is clear that one of the dominating features of galactic
synchronization is the Milky Way which has its own, significant place in both the mythology and the prophecies.
It is this we shall now consider.

### SUMMARY

The prophecy is of a sign which marks the moment of
turning towards a new 'Sun' or World Age. The sign is the
visible conjunction of the Sun with the Milky Way,
understood by the Maya to be the Tree of Life. In more
immediate terms, the most important aspect of this

prophecy is that the coming galactic synchronization will produce specific 'energy' effects; we shall return to this critically important subject of 'energies' in Prophecies 16 and 17. For the present we should note that their effects will be the direct result of the galactic synchronization outlined above.

# PROPHECY RELATED TO THE MILKY WAY

*The ceiba tree of abundance is their arbour ...*
*the first tree of the world was rooted fast.*

**Chilam Balam of Chumayel** [54]

## THE MESSAGE

In Mayan mythology the Milky Way, called the Ceiba tree, was understood as the Tree of Life. What will occur in 2012 is that the winter solstice Sun will conjunct with the 'Dark Rift' of the Milky Way which will rim the horizon as though lying on the Earth.

The mythology and prophecies associated with the Milky Way are multilayered; it was taken to be the Mayan World Tree, or Tree of Life, the source of life itself; it was seen as a road, a river, a Cosmic Mother and, of special significance, as a snake represented in Mayan art as a double-headed serpent or rattlesnake, with the Pleiades forming its tail. Of particular interest was the path of precession that would carry the Sun to meet the Milky Way. The conjunction of these two is sometimes represented as a cross similar to the Christian symbol. Although this astronomic image was exploited by the Spanish missionaries, it has nothing to do with Christianity. It is not seen by the Maya as a cross, but as the Cosmic Tree which, at the point of galactic synchronization on 21 December 2012, will form the very centre of the galaxy. This will be a unique event in recorded human history, an event that last took place approximately, 26,000 years ago.

The Maya noted that the Milky Way has a dark cleft running down the middle of it which is frequently referred to as the 'Dark Rift'. The name given to this by the Quiché Maya was *Xibalba*, the 'dark road' or the road to the underworld. To interpret the prophecy, modern Mayan elders use these mythic identities associated with the Dark Rift, which had several symbolic meanings that included: a cave mouth, a volcano's crater, the mouth of a frog-like cosmic monster, a jaguar or snake, a cleft in the Cosmic Tree itself, and as a phallic image of the Cosmic Mother's birth canal.[55] For the Maya, the source of all life was identified with the galactic or cosmic centre of the Milky Way, and in their mythology this was the 'Great Mother'. Her Dark Rift is the precise location where the December solstice Sun crosses the Milky Way and the mythology sees this conjunction as the sexual union of the First Father, the winter solstice Sun, with the First Mother, the Milky Way.

The Maya must also have considered the northern and southern polar stars as galactic centres, but it was the high-noon zenith passages of the Sun that presented a stronger case despite their variations according to latitude. From most Mayan sites, the Sun could be observed directly overhead illuminating a landscape without shadows. This occurred twice a year at the time of the spring and autumn equinoxes, when the Sun seemed to rise then set, due east and west. To this layer of the mythology must be added the concept of the Milky Way's conjunction with the Sun as a symbol of the Mayan Sacred Tree, or Tree of Life.

> At sunrise on December 21st 2012, for the first time in 26,000 years the Sun rises to conjunct the intersection of the Milky Way and the plane of the ecliptic. This cosmic cross is considered to be an embodiment of the Sacred Tree, the Tree of Life, a

tree remembered in all the world's spiritual
traditions.[56]

The Milky Way, as the Tree of Life, can be seen during late
summer when it turns on end taking the form of a tree.

It is precisely with the mythically fecund Dark Rift of the
Milky Way that a conjunction will be made with the plane
of the Sun's ecliptic. This mythology of the Milky Way as
the Great or Cosmic Mother and as the Tree of Life combine
to produce prophecies not of death but of birth, unity,
reconciliation (*see* Prophecy 11), the transformation of
human consciousness (*see* Prophecy 13), and a new relationship with Nature in its entirety (*see* Prophecy 14).

### SUMMARY

The prophecy for 2012 of the Milky Way forming the
symbolic tree-image, speaks of the continued evolution of
the entire planet and of everything that is dependent on it
for its life, both physically and spiritually. Aware that the
eventual alignment would take place at the end of the 13th
*baktun* (the 394-solar year block of time – *see* Appendix 4)
of the current cycle, the prophecy anticipates a major point
of transition in the history of planet Earth, the start of a
new World Age, and an unprecedented creative shift in
human consciousness and civilization.

# PROPHECY RELATED TO THE MOON

*Then when 5 Ahau arrived on his*
[the Year-bearer's] *day within the year 5*
*Muluc, there was a crescent Moon,*
*omen of life.*

Chilam Balam of Tizimin [57]

The Maya share with most other ancient cultures an obsessive mythological attachment to the Moon. They are alone, however, in giving the Moon its own calendar, the Tun-Uc, that plotted in detail, its movement and phases. Prophecy based on the Moon's astronomy and mythology speaks of unpredictably violent disasters such as flooding, and of humanity's wanton exploitation of the Earth's resources. Being the moody Moon, however, the prophecy has positive energies suggestive of creativity, and because of the Moon's association with weaving and agriculture, there are also functional and practical aspects.

❖

## COMMENTARY

The Maya's oldest astronomical records are the series of lunar glyphs that report the phases of the Moon. The prophecies associated with the Moon are, as with other planet-related prophecies, set against Mayan mythology and folklore, and tied to the Tun-Uc, the Mayan Moon calendar (*see* Appendix 6). The 'erratic' cycles of the Moon were counted as an alternation of 29 or 30 days, the mean average of 29.5 days integrating with their calendric system. The

Moon goddess has a chapter to herself in the Dresden Codex, and its accurate tables of Moon eclipse predictions is yet another example of the Maya's remarkable knowledge.

The prophetic significance of the Mayan lunar series is drawn from the way it is interrelated with the Tzolk'in, in which both images and text describe what is termed the 'burden' of the Moon goddess on the days of the Tzolk'in.

The point from which the Maya calculated the age of the Moon in any given cycle remains unclear, and varies between the dying of the old Moon and the birth of the new Moon. Calculating from the disappearance of the old Moon is still current among some Mayan village communities. What is apparent is that the Moon's age on any particular day, as it progresses from new Moon to new Moon, enforces the character of that day. We have already seen that this character will determine whether or not the day is auspicious for a specific activity (*see* Appendix 4). It is the character of the Moon goddess' 'burden' that gives each day its individual significance particularly with regard to those activities associated with her, such as childbirth, medicine and weaving. The Moon is therefore established at the most basic level of Mayan daily life, and its 'influence' takes us back into the realm of augury, in as much as these daily predictions provide a building-block foundation for the broader prophecy of, for example, a *katun*. But the lunar series have a more substantial contribution to make, since they enforce the theory that only the lunar calendar is in tune with 'natural time'. This important notion of 'natural time' is the substance of Prophecy 20.

Richard Tarnas tell us that the Moon is:

> the matrix of being, the psychosomatic foundation of the self, the womb and ground of life; ... that which senses and intuits; the feeling nature; the impulse and capacity to gestate and bring forth; ... the cycle of manifestation; the Great Mother Goddess, together with aspects of the Child constituting the relational matrix of life.[58]

So significant was the Moon and the lunar calendar that it had its own priesthood. The Jaguar Priest, the Chilam Balam of Tizimin, recorded the words of one such priest:

> Speaking as a Priest of the Moon, Nahau Pech declares, 'In those days there was understanding of the Moon ... in the time of our fathers ... This saying came from the mouth of Nahau Pech, the priest of the lunar calendar.'[59]

The determining influence of the Moon on the affairs of the Maya recurs in the writings of the Chilam, and the opening quotation for this Prophecy indicates its full significance: '*Then when 5 Ahau arrived on his day within the year 5 Muluc, there was a crescent Moon, omen of life.*' A later entry, for the prophecy of Katun 11 Ahau, the Moon's place in the event is made graphically clear:

> When the invasion came during Katun 11 Ahau,
> even the Heavens pitied themselves. They blamed
> it on the Moon when our warriors cut their own
> throats.[60]

A more mundane entry illustrates the extent to which the Moon directed the processes of agriculture:

> You say there is far too much whipping because
> you gather grain and other foods as you wish,
> according to the Moon, whether the Moon
> culminates in the signs of Taurus, Cancer, Virgo,
> Libra or Capricorn. All these signs rise occasionally
> for the sowing, and they are propitious for
> forming whatever it is you plant in the milpas.[61]

There are further references to the '*one who advises about new Moons*', and its association with rain, thus flooding.

In another part of the province there was a flood
of water. In great abundance it silently spread over
all creation … At new Moon they prayed for the
remnant of the days, for the remnant of the *katun*
afterwards.[62]

The Moon's ubiquitous but ambiguous influence is noted
by Chilam Balam of Chumayel:

This is the flower of the night … a star in the sky.
This is the vile thing of the night: it is the Moon.

Roys comments that for the Maya, the Moon's association
with the rabbit was a symbol of drunkenness, and with the
goddess, Tlacolteotl, with lust, or sinful love. The ominous
Moon-related predictions given for Katun 13 Ahau include
Christianized references to:

the universal judgement of our Lord God. Blood
shall descend from the tree and stone. Heaven and
Earth shall burn.

It is clearly a prophecy of the Maya succumbing to the new
religion, *'Great cities shall enter into Christianity … At the end of
our blindness and shame our sons shall be regenerated from carnal
sin.'* The *katun* prophecy concludes:

There is no lucky day for us. It is the cause of
death from bad blood, [probably dysentery] when
the Moon rises, when the Moon sets, the entire
Moon, this was its power; it was all blood.[63]

Inevitably, eclipses are a dominant feature in the calendars
and the prophecies based on them are wrapped around
eclipse mythologies. These show the Sun and Moon to be in
constant conflict, the eclipses being a figure of the battles
they wage. The Mayan word for 'eclipse', *chibil*, means 'eaten',
thus the Moon 'eats' the Sun, or the Earth 'eats' both of
them. One tradition tells of the people believing that, *xulab*,
ants, ate the Sun or Moon at the time of an eclipse.
However, the Chilam Balam of Chumayel offered a rational
explanation of the eclipse as a correction of this mythology,
but was not entirely successful, a case of the 'old, old, story'
prevailing. Much is read into this about the character of the
Moon; the Quiché Maya believed the Moon to be unpredictable, hard to understand, promiscuous and deceitful
and as such, was either the wife or mother of the Sun.
Various other titles were given to her, such as, 'Our Mother',
'Our Grandmother', and 'The Lady'. There will be two
eclipses of the Sun during 2012, the first being on May 20th
when the Sun and Moon will conjunct with Pleiades; this
will be visible in regions of Asia, the Pacific, and North
America, and as annular (when the Moon covers all but a

bright ring of the Sun) in China, Japan, the Pacific, and the western US. The second eclipse will occur on 13th November when the Sun and Moon will conjunct with the constellation Serpens, the Serpent; this will be visible in Australia, New Zealand, and South America, and as a total eclipse in Australia and the South Pacific.

There are many layers of meaning contributing to this prophecy. It is significant that more than with any other planet, Mayan mythology gives a very human character to the Moon, making much of its erratic behaviour, and its promiscuous and contentious nature. The Moon's influence is therefore unpredictable and unreliable. Yet, at the same time, the Moon has a mundane, practical significance as patron, for example, of weaving and childbirth. For understanding the prophecies, this human aspect is very important and needs to be considered independently of the complex mathematical and astronomical data that obscures the goddess' humanity. It must also be kept in mind that Mayan mathematics combines the cycles of the Moon with the 260-day cycle of the Tzolk'in; in addition, we also need to take into account that the day auguries and predictions accumulating towards a *katun* prophecy, rely as much on the 'human nature' of the Moon as on the 'burden' or character of each day. For the complete picture, the prophecies derived from the Moon must also be read with those for Venus (*see* Prophecy 9) and both in the context of the Tzolk'in.

## SUMMARY

The prophecy, associated with the cycles of the Moon's phases in the final *katun* ending in 2012, carry a message that is less than positive. The Moon's own character of deceitfulness, promiscuity and unpredictability, suggests events that will both surprise and challenge us. The Moon's association with water implies periods of disastrously destructive flooding. The familiar image of the 'man in the Moon' is seen by the Maya as the 'rabbit in the Moon' which carries the link with drunkenness, and thus of a humanity intoxicated with, for example, materialism, but in search of deeper satisfaction and contentment. In sharp contrast, the Moon's relationship to childbirth suggests a more positive outcome, perhaps the emergence of a new, sensitive and more cosmically conscious humanity. The extremes are clear, the outcome is in the balance.

- 9 -

# PROPHECY RELATED
# TO VENUS

*There they looked for the coming forth of the
Sun ... then they fasted and cried out in prayer.
They fixed their eyes firmly on their dawn,
looking there to the east. They watched closely
for the Morning Star, the Great Star that gives
its light at the birth of the Sun. They looked to
the womb of the sky and the womb of the Earth.*

**Popul Vuh** [64]

In Mayan mythology Venus is not anthropomorphized as the female symbol of erotic love, but as
the 'Dark Planet', the Mayan Mars, and also as a
manifestation of Quetzalcoatl. Malevolent and
violent gods were related to the morning and
evening star, and the cycles of Venus were
prescient of drought, danger and warfare. The
prophecy is clearly one of various forms of
impending conflict.

❖

## COMMENTARY

Another significant aspect of Mayan solar observation was
the ecliptic, that is, the observable path of the Sun, the
Moon and the planets, traced against the background of
the stars or constellations. However, it was the planet Venus
that interested the Maya most, being *of great importance to
the Maya as an object both of worship and of astronomical
exercises*.[65] The start-date of the Long Count Calendar, 13
August 3114 BCE, is sometimes referred to as the 'Birth of
Venus'; the end date, 21 December 2012, does not signify the
demise of Venus, but its earlier transition with the Sun on
6 June contributes significantly to the build-up towards
galactic synchronization (*see* Prophecy 6). That they

understood the morning and the evening star to be the same planet says much about the Mayan genius for astronomy and the extraordinary quality of their naked-eye observation. Much of this was undertaken at a unique circular building at Chichen Itza, known as the Caracol, which was built as an observatory specifically to record the movements of Venus. The extremely accurate data recorded there are contained in several codices, the fullest account being that of the Dresden Codex which is in the form of an almanac. It included five repetitions of the full cycle of Venus, that is, five sets of 584 days, or a total of 2,920 days, which is 8 years, together with the dates of its transit across the Sun. The Codex also includes almanacs for the movements of Mars and Jupiter, but it is Venus that dominates, and it was the only planet for which the Maya calculated extensive data.

For all her beauty, the Mexicans believed Venus was a malign influence most potent at the point of the heliacal rising. Bonewitz describes how, for the Maya:

> the one particular indicator of dark happenings
> was the rising or setting of Venus. Virtually unique
> among the astronomers of the ancient world, the
> Maya knew that the morning and evening stars
> were the same object, and made extensive and
> highly accurate studies of the movement of Venus.

> Why were particular astronomical conditions seen
> as so dangerous that they needed the offering of
> human life to prevent some dreadful occurrence?
> The answer must lie with some dreadful celestial
> event in the past, at a time when Venus was
> prominent to the Maya ... an event that affected
> many civilizations worldwide. ... Few celestial
> happenings could strike such terror into the
> hearts of men, but an impact of a comet or its
> fragments is certainly one of them.[66]

When the planet rose, the Mexicans, from earliest times, closed the doors and windows against its light which was believed to be unlucky and the bearer of sickness. The worst days were when the planet rose after an inferior conjunction when, depending upon the day, both people and nature would be threatened. The image given is of the rising of Venus being like a hurled spear, and a Mexican codex lists the 'spear's' targets on specific days as: the aged, the lords, the young, and rain, which was predictive of drought. There were times, however, when the planet's rising was the occasion of a positive augury. What is clear is that the Maya absorbed these earlier Mexican perceptions of Venus, and that the planet exerted an influence which determined the day's character and predictive potential.

Because Venus was the Mayan Mars, and their symbol of

war, the most auspicious dates for military initiatives were decided by the planet's position. Mayan inscriptions record that the moment of the appearance of the evening star was the signal for an attack on a city. Here we have the original 'star wars', and such battles, increasing in frequency during the 8th century CE, were the fiercest and bloodiest in Mayan history, and may well have contributed to the collapse of their Classical period civilization. The practice of excessive human sacrifice is sometimes explained as the conquering city making offerings to the gods during a conjunction of Venus. It is likely that the need for a supply of humans to sacrifice was the main cause of inter-city warfare, each army endeavouring to take prisoners that would be offered in sacrifice (*see* Introduction). The higher the rank of a captive, the more efficacious the sacrifice would be, the ultimate prize being the king, or ruler himself. One royal prisoner, *'the ruler Siebal, was kept alive for 12 years in order to be sacrificed at a particular conjunction of Venus.'* [67]

The sense of Venus as the 'dark' planet is thought to be due to its association with a catastrophic event in early Mayan history, such as comet impact, or massive flooding, which occurred at the time of a Venus transit. Prophecies of similar events would then be read into the future reappearances of Venus accurately recorded in the almanacs, and these would have been tied in to the repetition of the *katun* during which the original event took place. The catastrophe would have resulted in a massive loss of human life which was seen as a 'requirement' of the Venus-linked event. It is likely then, that the reason for such drastic measures as unsolicited human sacrifice, was to prevent a recurrence of a similar catastrophe.

Venus was believed to be a manifestation of Quetzalcoatl. It is a graphic image, since the god had sacrificed himself by plunging into the fire, as Venus seemingly does when it transits the Sun. In the mythology, Quetzalcoatl becomes the planet Venus and its appearances and reappearances are a figure of the birth-death-rebirth cycle. Thus prophecies associated with the return, or second coming, of Quetzalcoatl (*see* Prophecy 4) are linked to the cycles of Venus. The transit of Venus across the face of the Sun is an event that occurs in pairs, usually around eight years apart; the two last paired transits occurred in 1761/1769 and 1874/1882. In this final *katun* of the final *baktun* of the present age, a transit took place on 8 June 2004, and a second will be observable on 6 June 2012. Clearly, this event is part of a build-up towards the climax of galactic synchronization at the winter solstice in 2012.

### SUMMARY

The prophecy related to Venus, specifically as it transits the Sun, speaks of a critical period of transition both for our planet and humanity. The prophecy clearly recalls the original catastrophe that characterized Venus as the 'Dark Planet', and the practice of human sacrifice as a means to ward off the planet's violent and negative influences. The implication for our own, final *baktun* is that those dying in war might be thought of as having been 'offered' in sacrifice, the necessary price to be paid for the preservation of our civilization. In a broader sense, the prophecy calls for self-sacrifice, not suicide but restraint, in the face of the problems facing our society and planet. To balance this somewhat austere prognosis, we can refer to that aspect of the build-up to galactic synchronization at the winter solstice of 2012 when, on 6 June, Venus will transit the Sun. Because of the planet's association with Quetzalcoatl, the transit is to be understood as a visible appearance of the Feathered Serpent. For contemporary Mayan elders this points to 'Cosmic Initiation' (*see* Prophecy 13) and the time when solar sunspot activity will be at its maximum and generating other forms of energy on Earth (*see* Prophecy 17).

– 10 –

# THE PROPHECY OF TRANSITION TO A NEW AGE

*Then creation dawned upon the world. During the creation thirteen infinite series [steps] added to seven was the count of the creation of the world. Then a new world dawned for them.*

**Chilam Balam of Chumayel** [68]

The Mayan fifth World Age is drawing to a close; the sixth will begin in 2012. This marks the start of a new Great Cycle of time and the resetting of the clock of precession. We are, thus, between ages, a period known as the 'Apocalypse', meaning a time of revelation or disclosure. The prophecy combines with others that speak of the recovery of ancient wisdom, the assimilation of new truths, and the opportunity humanity will have to work out its problems responsibly, by the choices it makes.

## COMMENTARY

The transition of our civilization into a new age is a theme running through the Mayan prophecies and is probably the most familiar of them. The energy for the prophecy is derived from Mayan astrology (*see* Introduction), which in its modern form has kept us mindful of the astrological ages which are believed to mark progressive and significant changes in the development of humanity. The astrological age is determined by the precession of the equinoxes, a cycle of approximately 26,000 years (*see* Prophecy 6). What is termed 'The Great Year of Pisces' ran from 25300 BCE to 500 CE, during which Neanderthal man became extinct, Homo sapiens emerged, and the Mayan Long Count Calendar found its start-date in 3114 BCE. The present Great Year, which began in 500 CE, will conclude in 26300 CE, and the 'New Age' of Aquarius will begin sometime between 2060 CE to 2100 CE. However, we are already under the 'orb of influence of Aquarius' which, it is suggested, will guide humanity's escape from the confines of the Earth (its cradle) and its journey out into the universe. What this aspect of the prophecy speaks of, is a new migration that will settle other planets as once the great tribal migrations settled regions of the Earth.

Astrology apart, it is important to understand that the Mayan prophecy of a New Age does not stand alone, but resonates with other traditions, such as Vedic Hinduism's life-cycles of the Earth which are of 24,000 years duration. Each cycle was divided into four *yugas*, or ages of varying lengths, the Kali Yuga, a dark, materialistic age; the Dwapara Yuga, electrical or atomic age; the Treta Yuga, the mental age; and the Satya Yuga, the age of truth or enlightenment. In Hindu thought we are now in the Dwapara Yuga of electronics, atomic energy and technology, or what Argüelles' calls, the 'Technosphere'. Buddhism has world cycles corresponding to various mental states, such as desire, anger and fear, purity and trance, the cycles charting the karma-influenced spiritual evolution of the individual and humanity. Judaism looks to the 'Messianic Age', Christianity to its fulfilment with the second coming of Jesus. The Mayan prophecy of a New Age is therefore consistent with the collective perception of other established spiritual energies.

The Mayan elders understand that we are, at present, between worlds, and that during this 'apocalyptic' period two things will happen. The first is that new truths will be revealed through the rediscovery of Mayan wisdom (*see* Prophecy 2) and the second is that we will have the chance, both individually and collectively, to re-order our priorities, and by arriving at and effecting the right decisions, resolve the problems facing planet Earth (*see* Prophecy 16). This is the agenda for the apocalyptic interim period leading to 2012 and the start of a New Age. In a sense, humanity is therefore on trial, currently working out its salvation 'with fear and trembling'.

That the world is actually moving towards its physical end is doubtful, but this possibility needs to be considered (*see* Prophecy 15). Even if the destruction of the world is not yet on the agenda, our passage to and beyond 2012 may not be easy, since:

the polluted energy of the collective
unconsciousness will turn against humanity.
Whatever happens, it will be an expression of the

energy that is radiated by a humanity that is unable to live in peace and to make the right choices for peace, welfare, health and inner spirituality.[69]

However, the consensus among scholars suggests that while our transit between the Age of Pisces and Aquarius will be difficult, even threatening, the New Age offers a hugely positive potential involving profound changes at every level of life (*see* Prophecies 16, 17, 18, 19 and 20). The great Hindu guru Swami Sri Yukteswar (1855–1936) prophesied that the Atomic Age, the Dwapara Yuga referred to above, is a new ascending age in the life of our planet, during which we are destined to witness far-reaching changes in our religious, social, economic and political institutions.[70] His is an independent prophecy entirely in accord with that of the Maya.

Contemporary Mayan elders who have recovered and are disseminating the ancient wisdom, teach that this interim period is given to us as an opportunity to heal our abuse of the planet, to reconcile our antagonisms, and to work harmoniously for the future. The calendars (*see* Appendices) indicate that we are passing through the 13th and final 394-solar year *baktun* cycle which, according to the prophecies, would be characterized by 'the triumph of materialism', and 'the transformation of matter'. During this last *baktun*, which began approximately in 1618 CE and which will end in 2012 CE, humanity has become increasingly disconnected from the primal energies of Nature, thus severing itself from the natural energies on which people best thrive.

## SUMMARY

Our transition towards a New Age offers us a period of probation during which we have the opportunity to make the decision to improve and stabilize our relationships, and to accept our responsibility for the Earth. It is only by making such positive choices, that we can begin to solve the problems we face. In Mayan cosmology, the New Age signifies the creation of a new world; hopefully, this will mean regeneration for humanity and the planet's ecology.

# THE PROPHECY OF THE
# UNITY OF MANKIND

*Sufficient unto themselves are my words, for I
am Chilam Balam, the Jaguar Priest. I repeat
my words of divine truth: I say that the
divisions of the Earth shall be one! This is the
ninth year of Katun I Ahau.*

Chilam Balam of Tizimin [71]

*O Children of the people of the dawn,
O children of the people of the book, I come to
you as the special witness of time to remind you,
especially on the day of truth, that in your
origin you are one, and on the day of truth
you are to make yourselves one again.*

Pacal Votan [72]

## THE MESSAGE

It is prophesied that as we move towards 2012, it will become increasingly apparent that the various races, religions, and classes that divide us, mask an essential unity, and that despite the conflicts, people will be drawn closer together. The prophecy emphasizes that only by realizing our inherent unity can the problems now facing both our planet and our civilization be solved.

✦

## COMMENTARY

It has been said that as the things of the world break up, the things of the spirit gather together. In the face of our accumulating problems and the threat to the Earth (*see* Prophecies 15, 16, 17 and 19), the prophecy of unity is positive and optimistic. The Mayan elders regard this prophecy as already in the process of being fulfilled; they teach that there is now urgent need for races to unite, and for the barriers of religion and nationality to be transcended. In recent times there have been many initiatives taken to bring about the actual, rather than the implicit unity of mankind. Considerable problems remain, but there are signs of positive energies in political, religious, racial and community life. Paramahansa Yogananda believed that:

All the world's great religions are based on
common universal truths, which reinforce rather
than conflict with one another ... I have often said
that if Jesus, Krishna, Buddha, and other true
emissaries of God came together, they would not
quarrel, but would drink from the same cup of
God-communion.[73]

Throughout the 20th century Christianity has been
challenged by the ecumenical movement; similar initiatives
have been made within Judaism, and despite the fractured
nature of Islam, Muslims concerned with genuine spirituality have attempted reconciliation between, for example,
the Shiite and the Sunni. But the unity of which the
prophecy speaks is a far broader vision than the healing of
sectarian and denominational divisions within the separate
religions. It points to a more outward-looking interfaith
dialogue and mutuality (see Prophecies 4, 5 and 18).

The most advanced ancient and spiritual
traditions of the West and East, the Mayan and
Vedic, have been unified in a common framework
for understanding the future of humanity.[74]

There are many indications that this prophecy is in the
process of being fulfilled; the World's Parliament of

Religions had its inaugural meeting as long ago as 1893, with a further conference held in 1993 to commemorate the centenary. Subsequently there have been regular similar conferences held. The Council for a Parliament of World Religions is one of the principal agencies promoting interfaith dialogue. Its website mission statement reads like the mandate for the Mayan prophecy of unity:

> to cultivate harmony among the world's religious and spiritual communities and foster their engagement with the world and its other guiding institutions in order to achieve a peaceful, just, and sustainable world.[75]

The Council's agenda also takes up other priorities which resonate with the prophecies. Rowan Williams, the Archbishop of Canterbury, has advanced the quest for inter-religious dialogue through the Interfaith Initiative. There is no intention to bring all religions into a bland uniformity; the movement is concerned to focus on essential truth that, at heart, the various religions share a common quest and need not feel threatened by each other. Such energies do, indeed, suggest that the prophecy of unity is in the early stages of being fulfilled.

It is significant that Tibetan lamas were present in the pilgrimage to Chichen Itza, led by Hunbatz Men in March

1995. The event was also attended by the Wisdom Conservancy, an organization which promotes the culture and sacred knowledge of various indigenous people in the world. These initiatives are a part fulfilment of Prophecies 2 and 3 which we have already considered. Through the ceremonies led by elders, those present were asked to commit themselves to furthering the unity of humanity. Ceremony thus became a bridge that closed '*the gap between the continents, religions, cultures and races ... and to stand in peace as true sons and daughters of Cosmic Light*'.[76]

In considering the prophecy of Venus (*see* Prophecy 9), we noticed that the planet's transits of the Sun occur in pairs separated by eight years. The time between the transits is thought to be a 'doorway' through which an energy for unity may pass. It is a kind of cushion period, during which humanity has the chance to work for the reconciliation of all opposed and divided groups. The posts of the doorway are the two transits of Venus which, as we have seen (Prophecy 9) is, for the Maya, a planet associated with violent natural catastrophe and war. This means, of course, that the 'openness' of the opportunity may be impeded by periods of turbulence, darkness and destruction as old habit-conditioned forms of human consciousness change.

What will move people to transcend their conditioned separation is the recovery of memory (*see* Prophecy 14) and the retrieval of forgotten wisdom. The message of the prophecy is not confined to our need to overcome traditionally entrenched differences, but calls us also to be 'at one' with Nature and the universe.

> It is this very Earth we inhabit, linked with Heaven above us. Only in this setting can the mutuality and communality of the human race be newly created, with reverence and gratitude for that which transcends each of us singly, and all of us together. The authority of a world democratic order simply cannot be built on anything else but the revitalized authority of the universe.[77]

The paradigm of horizontal vision, of looking across at the other and feeling threatened, will be replaced by a vertical view; people will look upwards and away from themselves so as to take in the more extensive vision of our solar system and the energies that enable it to function. This renewed sense of space will be accompanied by a new sense of time. The unity of mankind will be made apparent as we rediscover the cyclical nature of time (*see* Prophecy 20), which is fully consistent with the rhythms of nature and the cyclical movements of the Sun, Moon and the planets. The prophecy indicates that during this period, humanity, also, will come full circle.

I am Another Yourself.

*Lak'ech*, the Yucatec Mayan Code of Honour

#### SUMMARY

The message of the prophecy is a stark reminder of Benjamin Franklin's warning, '*we must indeed all hang together, or, most assuredly we shall all hang separately*'. Humanity is fighting its battle on two fronts, the one being to prevent the collapse of our own civilization, the other to prevent the terminal spoliation of our planet. The only possible way to resolve these problems is for a globally concerted effort to be made. Hope lies in the evidence indicating that the prophecy of unity and reconciliation is already in the early stages of being fulfilled.

# THE PROPHECY OF A NEW 'ENLIGHTENMENT'

*Your souls shall accept the truth and hold it in high esteem ... It will come to pass that you shall adore the divine truth, and the government of our ancestors will stand in readiness forever.*

The Prophecy of Yuban Chan, The Book of Chilam Balam of Tizimin [78]

## THE MESSAGE

The main thrust of the prophecy's message is the need for a radical shift in our perception and understanding, especially with regard to our relationship with Nature and our place within the universe. Enlightenment resonates with cosmic wisdom (*see* Prophecies 2, 13 and 14), and the prophecy of such an enlightenment being realized in this age is exciting and optimistic.

## COMMENTARY

The astronomical transition leading to galactic synchronization which, according to the Mayan calendar, we are now undergoing, will move us from the 'Age of Belief' to the 'Age of Knowledge'. This new knowledge, the sources of which are to be found in Mayan indigenous culture was, as we have seen, hidden (*see* Prophecy 2), but has been recovered by contemporary Mayan elders. The transition from 'belief' to 'knowledge' will result in a radical change in our perceptions, and the prophecy speaks of this being effected by 'enlightenment'. The prophet of the Book of the Jaguar Priest affirmed that, gradually, humanity, '*will begin to esteem our learning and our knowledge of the unrolling of the face of the universe ...*'.[79] The fulfilment of the prophecy of enlightenment is, in part, being realized by the initiatives of two Mayan elders, Hunbatz Men, a day-keeper and founder of the Mayan Indigenous Community, and Don Alejandro Oxlaj, a seventh-generation priest from Guatemala and Head of the Maya Elder Council. The initiation ceremonies Hunbatz Men conducted, for example, on the spring equinox of 1995 at Chichen Itza, were designed to lead those present to a shift in consciousness that amounted to enlightenment.

It is important to keep in mind that prophecies of a new enlightenment are not limited to the Maya, nor are the teaching initiatives confined to the elders. Other traditions corroborate that the Mayan prophecy speaks of a global energy now gathering considerable momentum. One striking example of this is Sri Bhagavan Kalki, believed by many to be the living avatar of Kalki:

> Around Kalki [Sri Bhagavan], an enlightenment
> avatar in south India, prophecies have emerged
> that if humanity is to survive, it needs to attain the
> enlightenment state by the year 2012. From the
> perspective of the Mayan calendars certain aspects
> of this development in the East are remarkable. To
> begin with, Kalki himself was born on day 13 Ahau
> [7 March 1949] which in the Mayan calendar
> generates the prophesied energy of enlightenment.

Secondly, Kalki's teaching about the deadline for the enlightenment of humanity by the year 2012, is an independently arising confirmation of the validity of the Mayan calendar's deadline for the completion of the cosmic plan. [80]

Like the Mayan elders, Kalki speaks of the urgent need for a new enlightenment. In Hindu mythology the god Kalki is the tenth and final avatar of Vishnu the Preserver, and prophecies of his return date back to the 7th century CE. The Hindus also speak of an 'age of darkness and destruction' that Kalki's return will bring to an end. He is known also as the destroyer of filth, confusion and ignorance. It is significant that *'kalki'* is also as a metaphor for 'time' and 'eternity'. As the avatar of Kalki, Sri Bhagavan Kalki teaches a message uncannily similar to the Mayan elders: Humanity is entering the most crucial phase of its existence, and the coming years will witness the unprecedented and undreamt-of changes in the course of its long evolution. There is nothing much humanity can do about it, other than to understand the overpowering changes that will occur, and to flow with them. Towards the end, humanity will enter a New Age, the 'Golden Age' (*see* Prophecy 10), the transition to which will be a painful process. Only those whose relationships are in order will pass through it easily. Other, similar 'enlightenment' messages include

Paramahansa Yogananda's call to self-realization, and the 'enlightenment' message of Buddhism which is attracting so much attention in the West.

It is prophesied that during this 'between worlds' apocalypse, people can expect to undergo personal changes, as many and varied as the people experiencing them. The way through these changes could be traumatic and radical, and may include the ending of relationships and the establishing of new ones, a change of residence, or a change of career which might require relocation. Of more significance is that enlightenment implies, or requires, a radical shift in the way we think, with the result that our conditioned concepts will be challenged and reformed, and the received traditions of our ideas and the habits they nurture, reconstructed. Such changes will lead to new values, priorities, perceptions and thus, to a critical examination of individual and collective behaviour.

The consequences of reformed habits of thought are far-reaching, since our conscious patterns of thought are paralleled by changes in our unconscious mind which, in turn, reflects physical patterns in the outer world.

> In particular, as psychic patterns are on the point
> of reaching consciousness, then synchronicities
> reach their peak; moreover, they generally
> disappear as the individual becomes consciously

aware of a new alignment of forces within his or her own personality. It is as if the internal restructuring produces external resonance, or as if a burst of 'mental energy' is propagated outward into the world.[81]

This enlightened change in our ways of thinking, will echo those of the Maya for whom there was little difference between the material and spiritual world. This itself is a radical and liberating perception, of equal importance to the prophecies as is the concept of time being cyclic. The result of this enlightenment is that we shall begin to understand, as did the Maya, that 'gods' represent the forces of nature and human feelings and emotions, and that myth has the power of concrete reality; that both the spiritual and the material are scanned by the senses in exactly the same way as are the incalculable dimensions of space and time; that the 'way to the stars' is not therefore conceived by an excess of imagination, but perceived as a path followed by the senses, that is through every 'sensible' category by which a human being lives. Enlightenment will also help us to realize that the mental, or 'conscious', is also a property of matter. This important idea is one we shall develop under the next prophecy.

SUMMARY

The enlightenment of which the prophecy speaks includes the concept of 'awakening' to the truth that is also at the heart of Eastern mysticism. But the Mayan teachers do not expect this to be a matter of sudden, or immediate perception. This will certainly be the experience of some, but for most of us it will happened more gradually, through a process of teaching and reflection. It will be a progressive revelation, a slow dawning that, eventually, will touch everyone.

# THE PROPHECY
# OF COSMIC
# CONSCIOUSNESS

*Only through the solar initiation can
the sleeping body of mankind be awakened ...
Let us prepare to receive the light of knowledge
that comes from Hunab K'u, and transcend into
the memory of the Creator and become beings
of eternal luminosity.*

The Sacred Manuscript of K'altun [82]

This prophecy of K'altun carried to us by the contemporary Mayan Elder, Hunbatz Men, speaks of the coming of the 'time of knowledge', 'transcendence' and 'luminosity'. By initiation, humanity will recover an atavistic perception of the universe. The prophecy recalls us to the central Mayan precept that *everything* is energy, and of our urgent need to be conscious of it as the driving principle of the universe, and to experience it in its innumerable manifestations.

❖

## COMMENTARY

It is prophesied that initiation in cosmic wisdom is for future initiates. These will come from every part of society, to include the young and the old, both men and women, who have realized that our materialistic civilization is failing to meet its educational responsibilities and has had a regressive effect on our spirituality. 'Cosmic consciousness' is a term widely used by both Western and Eastern mystics and philosophers, and by primordial, ancient, and New Age religions. Scaruffi's⸍ perceptive concept of the mental being a property of matter saves the concept from being an esoteric mystical idealism. It recalls us to the central Mayan notion that everything in the entire observable universe is energy.

What is 'cosmic consciousness'? It is a form of focused mindfulness that enables the individual to feel in tune with the life and order of the universe. It is not merely an intellectual concept, and it goes far beyond simply holding the idea in one's mind that everything is a part of the whole and has its proper place. Cosmic consciousness is the actual *experience* of that sense of personal unity with the cosmos that transcends the limiting, but dominant, awareness of the 'self', which tends to focus on our personal identity. It can be argued that such an experience is the goal of all religions, and that traditionally the realization of cosmic consciousness has been confined to mystics.

The experience is an integral part of Mayan religion, and the prophecy suggests that during this period of radical change, there will be an increasing number of those who will be so enlightened (*see* Prophecy 12). Every human being can, by birthright, achieve cosmic consciousness, but the teaching tells us that some form of initiation or guidance is helpful. It is beyond the scope of this book to explore the forms of initiation offered by the Maya and other religions. But because of the central place of the Sun in Mayan cosmogony it is useful to notice the references to 'solar initiation' of the kind Hunbatz Men led at the spring equinox of 1995 (*see* Prophecy 3). As a result of such initiations, the individual will be awakened, as if from sleep; humanity will be brought out from the shadow of its obsession with materialism by the 'the lightning flash' of Hunab K'u, the creator god. The Mayan astrologer and spiritual guide Aluna Joy Yaxk'in puts the matter simply:

> the human race will have to seek the path of initiation on Earth and in Heaven ... Through Solar Initiation they will be able to see the luminosity of the great spirit ... through Solar Initiation, the sleeping body of mankind can be awakened. Hunab K'u will flash like lightning that will pierce through the shadows that envelop the human race.[83]

All these phrases are familiar metaphysical terms. What we need to understand is that for the Maya, 'solar initiation' and its attendant images were part of a central truth and integral to their way of life. Furthermore, the prophecy points to the urgent need for humanity to reach for cosmic consciousness if it is to survive. 'Seeing the luminosity' is understood by the Maya as, *'the auspicious event of initiation into cosmic consciousness that will reawaken humanity into the Age of Knowledge'*.[84] Hunbatz Men speaks of a higher initiation:

According to High Initiation, it is written that the wisdom of the cosmic light will return. When the human race begins to slip into the darkness of ignorance, oblivion, and despair, it will be the wisdom of the seven brothers of our Father Sun that will shed the great light of wisdom in order to awaken the powers that have remained dormant in human beings due to an erroneous form of education. In this New Age, the Mysteries Schools have the responsibility of reclaiming a confused mankind and leading it through the path of the multicoloured light of cosmic education.[85]

As with the gods and mythology, the Maya did not regard this higher 'consciousness', or 'cosmic education', as metaphysical, but as a concrete aspect of everyday life. Their perception comes close to Piero Scaruffi's suggestion (as cited earlier in this commentary) *that a simple theory of consciousness can be advanced by accepting that the mental is a property of matter*.[86]

What the prophecy speaks of, is a form of consciousness that is different to our normal state of being and one to which we all have access.

Our normal waking consciousness, rational consciousness as we call it, is but one special type

of consciousness, while all about it, parted from it
by the flimsiest of screens, there lie potential
forms of consciousness entirely different. No
account of the universe in its totality can be final
which leaves these other forms of consciousness
quite disregarded.[87]

It is a form of consciousness that calls on an energy
associated with the deepest spirituality. Prophecy 18 is
concerned with continuing evolution, and genetic development; spiritual development will draw on an energy which
the history of spirituality has shown to be the greatest
power to which we have access. The American mathemati-
cian and electrical engineer Charles Steinmetz (quoted by
Paramahansa Yogananda*) believed that while humanity is
aware of this power it has '*been merely playing with it, and has
never seriously studied it as we have the physical forces*'.

The prophecy is also about carrying the wisdom
recovered by the Mayan elders (*see* Prophecy 2) to the whole
world in preparation for 2012; this, as we have seen, is also
being fulfilled. Confronting the world with the need for
cosmic consciousness is not just the responsibility of the
elders, '*it is also prophesied that this initiation of cosmic wisdom is
for future initiates,*'[88] who, as noted above, will be drawn from
a cross-section of society.

Clearly, consciousness of any kind is registered by

thought, and the way we think, the attitudes we have, determine the quality of our personal lives and that of the society in which we live. The gaining of cosmic conscious-ness will radically alter the matrix of our thinking patterns, (*see* Prophecy 12) something Teilhard de Chardin called the 'noosphere'.

> The idea is that of the Earth, not only becoming covered by myriads of grain of thought, but becoming enclosed in a single thinking envelope so as to form, functionally, no more than a single vast grain of thought on the sidereal scale.

Our initiation into cosmic consciousness is perhaps what he called 'psychical expansion', the one thing, he argues, that we lack, '*and it is staring us in the face if we would only raise our heads to look at it*'.[89]

### SUMMARY

The Maya understood that everything that exists is energy and consciousness is a property of matter. Thus, what appears to be a prophecy rooted in an abstract metaphysi-cal process is, in reality, far more concrete. The Mayan elders teach that during this inter-world period, it will be the choices we make that determine how we enter the next age, and that these choices will have real and practical consequences to the point of determining not only the quality of future life, but whether there will actually be a future. The prophecy speaks of the power of sharply focused collective thought – its potential may be the most powerful energy humankind has ever released.

– 14 –

# THE PROPHECY OF RECOVERED MEMORY

*A wave of disgust sweeps through the house of the gods because you forgot Life, you forgot your own ancient teaching.*

Chilam Balam of Tizimin [90]

## THE MESSAGE

The prophecy speaks of a collective spiritual amnesia from which our civilization suffers, and it refers, in modern terminology, to what is called 'recovered memory'. Once our memory of cosmic wisdom has been retrieved, we will have a deeper understanding of who we are, and of our relationship with Nature and the universe.

The prophecy speaks of a time in the earliest days of human evolution and development, when people related to Nature with a very different attitude to the one prevalent today. A person would have known, instinctively and intuitively, that each individual was an integral part of the whole matrix of life, and that there was an optimum way to live so as to realize the potential of this integration. The prophecy implies that civilization is both developed and sustained more by right thinking, by a certain kind of attitude and knowledge, than by the constructs of science and technology, and that the instinct and intuition that informed our knowledge has been lost, or at least obscured. The good news is that such knowledge is recoverable, not just as an idea or theory, but as an experience that supports a way of life.

This quest for the recovery of a special kind of knowledge is shared by most religions. This loss of knowledge, or awareness, is seen as one of the root causes of the problems we face, especially of the deep sense, so many seem to have, that 'something is missing', and that we are out of touch with an essential energy. In Christian tradition, this sense of lack is referred to as 'original sin', causing an inherent separation from God. The theology represents a truth broader than its own context, that many feel estranged or disconnected from a basic god-like essence. In Buddhism the sense of lack is the result of *avidya*, or ignorance. The prophecy reminds us that the truth of the matter lurks in our individual and collective memory, and that we have both the chance and the responsibility to recover the ancient wisdom that is our birthright. And the wisdom is, indeed, ancient, set down in the first beginnings of the civilizations from which the Maya evolved (*see* Introduction).

As we have noted, the Mayan insight is bound up in the relationship between astronomy, mathematics, and human nature, an interdependence made apparent in the range of calendars the Maya developed (*see* Appendices). More importantly, the knowledge was encoded as myths which were themselves an account of actual events that took place in the formative period of their existence. Mythology, and the oral tradition that carried it down the years can, thus, be read as tribal memory. We all carry vestiges of tribal memory in our subconscious, and the prophecy speak of the immanence of our recovery of the original truths of our identity.

As we have established, the Maya clearly prophesied both the Spanish conquest and their conversion to the new religion (*see* Prophecy 1). In one sense the loss of knowledge was actual and physical, being the destruction of nearly all the Mayan codices, an act that has been described as a 'cultural holocaust'. In another sense the knowledge was not lost, but 'hidden'. As custodians of this wisdom, the ancient confederation of Native American elders decided to 'hide' the wisdom, entrusting it to particular families. They have come together in times of crises across the centuries and, as we have seen, they were called, in 1995, to Chichen Itza by Hunbatz Men who, himself of that lineage, is a custodian and an inheritor of the wisdom. Events have shown that Prophecies 1, 2 and 3 are in the process of being fulfilled by the Maya's own recovery of the knowledge. This prophecy, however, speaks of a more general, even of a universal recovery of memory.

However, a problem remains. The Western mind is not capable of understanding the indigenous Mayan wisdom, but inevitably overlays it with its own perceptions and values. We have noted that extreme materialism is characteristic of the final *baktun* of this age of the Fifth Mayan Sun, the final *katun* of which will end in 2012. What this prophecy is warning us about, is that our spiritual amnesia is the consequence of materialism; it is as if humanity is plagued by a memory virus that has eroded the wisdom that is its birthright.

Once we have recovered the memory of our rightful place in the universe, together with our sense of unity with it, humanity will, once again, have the means of realizing its spiritual potential and of solving the problems with which it is faced.

Why do we remember the past and not the future?

Stephen Hawking, *A Brief History of Time*

### SUMMARY

The prophecy predicted that the final *baktun* would be a period of 'great forgetting', during which our proper relationship to, and sense of oneness with Nature would be lost. It also speaks of our recovery from this amnesia, as we regain the original insight and knowledge. Wisdom, or cosmic consciousness, is not the monopoly of any one culture or nation, but in history there are occasions when it is given to a people to be its custodians, so that when the time is auspicious, it can be recovered. The prophecy speaks of a coming memory revolution. The recovery of knowledge will '*enable people to echo the memory of the universe. And the new humankind will possess special capabilities, rationality and emotion.*' [91]

# THE PROPHECY OF THE DESTRUCTION OF THE EARTH

*When Katun 9 Ahau shall arrive later on,*
*then they must all profess my teachings, when*
*that day comes ... without forsaking them, in*
*the final days of misfortune, in the final days of*
*the tying up of the bundles of the thirteen*
*katuns on 4 Ahau, then the end of the world*
*shall come and the katun of our fathers will*
*ascend on high.*

**Chilam Balam of Tizimin** [92]

## THE MESSAGE

The end of each Mayan age, or Sun, is marked by extreme natural catastrophe. The current age, or Fifth Sun, will terminate in 2012, and it is prophesied that the Earth will experience violent earthquakes and volcanoes together with the side effects these produce. Either by sudden catastrophe such as comet impact, or the longer process of ecological deterioration, the possibility has to be considered that the Earth, itself, is at risk.

❖

## COMMENTARY

The prophecy carries the clear message of the Earth being at risk. As we have seen, the Maya believe we are nearing the end of the age of the Fifth Sun. The ending of the four previous ages of the Sun was marked by natural disaster caused successively by water, wind, fire and Earth changes; the Aztec Sun Stone carries glyphs telling of the four previous Suns brought to an end by wild animals, wind, fire and flood.

There is geological evidence to suggest that every quarter of the 25,600-year Long Count cycle (*see* Appendix 4), that is every 6,400 years, there has been a major physical crisis on Earth. The Mayan calendric records show that these events have taken the form of great floods, earthquakes, volcanoes, fires, and comet impact. Ancient texts, such as the Old Testament, have documented a 'great flood', and Plato recounted the story of the inundation that destroyed Atlantis. Each of these natural disasters reduced the Earth to a state of chaos, followed by a transitional period of regeneration as the 'new age' got underway.

However, there are interpreters who read the prophecy of the end of the fifth and final age, as a warning of the destruction of the Earth. On the precedent of what has happened at the conclusion of previous ages, this may mean the ending of the world 'as we know it'. This interpretation has a certain, compelling plausibility, since it is consistent with one of the dominant themes running through all the prophecies, that of radical change. Whatever form this might take, it is not clear whether this annihilation will be instant, or the result of a more gradual process. If 2012 marks the end of the planet, no one is suggesting that this will happen at midnight of the winter solstice; contemporary Mayan elders are predicting that the cataclysm may occur within a hundred years of this date, and that the energy for this would not be metaphysical or astrological, but astronomical. Whatever the scenario, it is clear that the prophecy requires us to give serious consideration to the possibility that the Earth, from whatever cause, is at risk.

The basis for this prophecy is the Mayan calendars. We

are living through the final *baktun* of 1618–2012 CE, that is the 13th *baktun* cycle characterized by 'the triumph of materialism' and 'the transformation of matter'. The prophecies based on the final 20-year period of Katun 4 Ahau are very varied, even contradictory, the emphasis depending on the sources used, and on the point of view of the interpreter. While the character of 'Ahau', meaning 'Lord,' suggests change, by virtue of it being set at the end of a *baktun*, it is also the *katun* of completion. In this sense, completion means not only the final working out of the *katun*'s own energies, but also the energies of all the Katun Ahaus preceding it. Katun Ahau is followed by Katun Cauac, meaning 'storm', itself a *katun* associated with the release and intensification of waves of energy making for change. What the calendric aspect of the prophecy is suggesting is that whatever happens around 2012, will do so because of the accumulating characteristics of the preceding 4 Ahau *katuns* since the beginning of the Long Count Calendar in 3114 BCE.

Don Alejandro Oxlaj (see p.112), a priest descended from the ancient Mayan priesthood, warns us that:

> There have always been destroyers. They destroy
> peace. They destroy the environment. They destroy
> the beauty of Mother Earth. They pollute space.
> Scientists say we have even ruptured the balance of

the Ozone layer. ... We do not have much time left. We have only 14 years until the year zero. [Written in 1998. Now, in 2008, we have only four years left.] After the year Zero there shall be peace. There shall be peace even if there are no survivors.[93]

Prophets of doom are not, of course, unprecedented. Such an eschatology, be it of a final battle between 'good' and 'evil', or of a Last Judgement of humanity presided over by an absolute, omnipotent deity, is a feature shared by the major dualistic religions. End-of-the-world, or Age mythologies are also built into many ancient, even proto-religious systems, for example that of the Germanic-Norse myth with its final battle of Ragnarok, the difference here being not that the world will end, but that the catastrophe will terminate one World Age only to give birth to another. It is of this kind of transition that the prophecies speak, the ending of one World Age and the start of another.

One strong contender responsible for the demise of the planet is comet, asteroid or meteorite impact. That the Earth has already suffered from these is beyond dispute. It is generally accepted that the dinosaurs were eliminated in this way, and according to the research of Dr Bill Napier, so were earlier civilizations such as those of the Egyptian Old Kingdom and Sumeria. Dr Napier of the Armagh Observatory, and Chandra Wickramasinghe of the Centre of Astrobiology at Cardiff University, have produced research suggesting that the risk of such impacts is higher than previously thought.[94] For this reason there is an urgent escalation of agencies responsible for finding and tracking near-earth asteroids, 'NEAs', and setting up contingency aid plans in the event of such an impact taking place.

The prophecy is not saying that on 21 December 2012, the Earth will be hit by a comet capable of destroying human civilization. Disaster there may be, but the Mayan priest and elder, Carlos Barrios, assures us by gentle rebuke that the prophecies are not about our annihilation:

> Anthropologists visit the temple sites and read the steles and inscriptions and make up stories about the Maya, but they do not read the signs correctly. It's just their imagination... Other people write about prophecy in the name of the Maya. They say that the world will end in December 2012. The Maya elders are angry with this. The world will not end. It will be transformed. The indigenous have the calendars, and know how to accurately interpret it, not others.[95]

## SUMMARY

Among the predicted causes of an Earth-threatening catastrophe, comet impact must remain a possibility, but we have to keep in mind that while some interpretations of the prophecies point to a massive global catastrophe, comet impact is only one of several possible causes. Others, as indicated above, are all associated with more local, natural occurrences. What the prophecy speaks of clearly, is that while a sudden, terminal end of the Earth is unlikely, we will have to work through the consequences of our spoliation of the planet, and of our exploitation of its natural resources. Most scholars of the Mayan calendric prophecies do not support the supposition that the end of the world is imminent, but the consensus is that we could be in for a rough ride and that we can expect to see *'chaos and destruction in all the kingdoms of nature'*.[96]

# PROPHECIES OF EARTH CHANGES, ECOLOGY, & CLIMATE

*The surface of the Earth will be moved. How can the people be protected, thus disturbed in the midst of the Earth, in the sculptured land of Ichcansiho. ... According to the omens above the Earth and the prophecies, the disturbances of our land shall eventually turn back.*

Chilam Balam of Tizimin [97]

The Maya prophesied that the time would come when we would be in conflict, rather than in harmony, with nature. Knowing that this period would coincide with the Saturn-Pluto cycle, they further prophesied that our being at variance with Nature would be a characteristic of the period through which we are now passing. The prophecy warns of the steadily degrading effects of pollution and natural disaster on the Earth's biosphere, that is on the crust or shell of our planet, including the air, land, all surface soil, sand, rock and water, in short, on all those elements of the Earth that support life. Despite the biospheric and spiritual crisis we face, the prophecy has an optimistic edge in anticipating the recovery of our sense of unity with Nature as we endeavour to solve the problems.

COMMENTARY

The threat to the Earth and the life it sustains is a major theme of the Mayan prophecies for 2012, and one that for many years has been the subject of world media attention. To that extent, the prophecy that we will become increasingly aware of the problem and will set out to solve it, is already being fulfilled. There is no necessity here to heighten the ecological emergencies we face, other than to reflect on climate change, the melting icecaps (which may be part of a completely natural cycle), and the extinction of forms of life, which is running at about 1,000 species per year, greater than at any time since the extinction of dinosaurs 65 million years ago. For this loss of flora and fauna, we must accept most of the responsibility.

In addition, the threat of oil shortage is the main cause of an approaching energy crisis, made more urgent and dangerous because the major sources of oil are situated in regions of political instability. It has been estimated that the supply of oil will last only until around 2050; although we are aware of the problem we are ill prepared for it and the suddenness with which it will come.

> The effects of such a crisis could be exponentially magnified by the side effects of accelerated climate change, resource depletion, military conflicts, and declining food production.[98]

The prophecy warns of the consequence of our exploitation of the planet's resources, and to a sudden escalation of this world-wide energy crisis. In order to heal the damage we have caused, we will need to bring the biosphere into full relationship with what Teilhard de Chardin called the 'noosphere' (from the Greek *'nous'* meaning 'mind', *see* p.123) or with what, for Plato, was the rational part of the soul. De Chardin, like the Mayan elders before him, called for a kind of ecumenicity of thought, a *'plurality of individual reflections grouping themselves together and reinforcing one another in the act of a single unanimous reflection'*.[99]

In a broadcast on 10 January 2005, Mitch Battros reported the warning of the Mayan elder Carlos Barrios:

> Through the ancient techniques of divination and tools of prophecy, the Mayan elders are calling forth to pay close attention to messages being set forth by ongoing Earth-changing events. ... The message is not meant to induce fear, but to give warning of preparation and to remain aware of your surroundings. The elders are concerned about what has been presented in their recent divinations and they call to all humanity to warn their leaders and to work very hard at a spiritual level to prevent the impending destruction.[100]

The prophecy of Earth changes is less alarming than those pointing to the end of the world itself, but no less challenging. The consensus among Mayan elders and day-keepers is that all Earth-related prophecies are concerned with a process, rather than with a one-off final catastrophe. However violent these events, they will be the consequences of these prophesied Earth changes.

Over many years we have witnessed the rise, both in number and strength, of hurricanes, cyclones and tornadoes. The attention of the whole world was riveted on the Indian Ocean tsunami of 26 December 2004, caused by the Sumatra-Andaman earthquake. Noted also, is an increase in the number of exceptionally violent volcanic eruptions such as that of Mount St Helens on 18 May 1980. It was recorded as the most lethal and economically destructive volcanic event in the history of the United States, but some agencies suggest that hurricane Katrina and the flooding of New Orleans in August 2005, has superseded it. More threatening than any of these is the colossal, 'super volcano' lying under America's Yellowstone National Park which, if it erupts, could threaten the human race with extinction. The Mayan elders regard such natural disasters as a vindication of the prophecy's warning about the release of natural and destructive energies. We have seen that the sudden collapse of Mayan civilization occurred during a *katun* characterized by changes to the Earth. While these do not adequately account for the demise of their civilization, they most certainly contributed to it.

Don Alejandro Oxlaj, the Mayan priest referred to above, warns that *'the Sun will be hidden for a period of 60–70 hours and this is when we shall enter the period of the Fifth Sun'.*[101] The loss of the Sun for two or three days is a clear indication of some kind of natural disaster such as the ash cloud of a violent volcanic eruption, which, while not a threat to the entire human race, indicates radical Earth changes at a local or national level.

## SUMMARY

The prophecy speaks of our exploitation of the Earth, and our pollution of the biosphere as a feature of the period of time leading to 2012. Opinion remains divided about the extent to which industry and scientific and technological advances, have contributed to global warming and climate change, since these, especially the latter, may well be part of natural cycles of change over a very long period of time. Returning this critical prophecy of Earth changes to Mayan calendric astronomy, we can say the Earth has entered the final phase, or katun of the Great Cycle 1992 to 2012, a period leading to the Earth's conjunction with the Milky Way. The Maya call this the 'Earth Regeneration Period', when as a result of that conjunction the planet will begin to cultivate a new and complete 'purity'.

We can but hope.

- 17 -

# THE PROPHECY OF CHANGES TO THE EARTH'S MAGNETIC FIELD

*Again the time of the Mayan cosmic education has come. Thousands of years ago, the sacred teachings from the cosmos were deposited in many magnetic centres throughout the world:* [For example] *Chan Chan (Peru), Tulle (France), Hu-nan (China), Bethlehem (Israel), Tih (Egypt), Mississippi (United States), Humac (Brazil), Nagasaki (Japan), and Mull (Scotland). The names of all these places are of Maya origin, which confirms that, in different periods of times, the Maya were present in these sacred magnetic centres.[102]*

Hunbatz Men

### THE MESSAGE

The prophecy speaks of the relationship between Mayan wisdom and magnetic centres. More specifically, it points to unprecedented and violent sunspot activity that will cause a radical change in the Earth's magnetic field, perhaps amounting to a reversal of the poles. The Maya charted such activity over a period of 5,126 years, the current cycle of which is that of the Long Count Calendar, 3114 BCE to 2012 CE.

✦

### COMMENTARY

The Maya feared that at the end of each Age of the Sun, the Sun itself would decline and be unable to support life on the planet. What is prophesied is not the decline of the Sun, but a radical change in its behaviour which will have dramatic consequences for the Earth. An early sign of the prophesied change in the Sun's activity is a reversal of the Earth's magnetic field. Because of the galactic synchronization (*see* Prophecy 6) that occurs at the winter solstice of 2012, the Maya believe the Sun will receive some form of extra energy that will intensify its own light. Scientists know these intensifications to be sunspots or solar flares, and that they affect the Sun's own magnetic field. Because this has a knock-on effect on Earth, it causes a displacement in the Earth's rotation which may result in various forms of natural disasters. Throughout the history of the Earth, the magnetic poles have been frequently reversed; such a change in the Sun's magnetic energy is thought to have set up a sequence of solar activity begun in 2000 CE, which will reach a climax in 2012. The Maya charted these changes over periods of 5,126 years, that is the period of their Long Count Calendar, the current one beginning as we have noted, in 3114 BCE and concluding in 2012 CE.

Lest it be thought that these immense physical changes to the Sun and the Earth are simply a matter of whimsical speculation, it should be noted that this prophecy is validated by NASA.[103] In the first place, NASA predicts that there will be a very intense solar storm in 2012, with the sunspot cycle rising to a new maximum with the increased activity 30–50 per cent greater than previous storms. Secondly, NASA predicts that the Sun will also reverse its own magnetic poles during 2012 as a result of reaching the end of the current 11-year sunspot cycle. Some scientists believe this will amplify the effects of retarding the magnetic field on Earth, as harmful particles blasted away from the Sun would more easily penetrate the Earth's atmosphere. What is a solar storm? The storm that affects Earth is called a geomagnetic storm which causes temporary disturbances in the Earth's magnetosphere. As a result of solar flares, solar wind shock-waves strike the Earth's magnetic field only 24 to 36 hours after the event on the Sun.

To interpret the prophecy of changes in the Earth's magnetic field, we need to take into consideration Maurice Cotterell's theory [104] relating astrology to Sun cycles, which he first developed in 1986 while working as the Head of Electrical and Communications Engineering at Cranfield Institute of Technology. He constructed a computer programme that would correlate the relationship between the Sun's magnetic field and the Earth. The model confirmed the long observed 11½-year cycle of sunspot activity. Of more significance was the evidence computed for much longer cycles one of which was of 1,366,040 days. Cotterell noticed that the difference between this number, and the Mayan 'super number' of the Dresden Codex, 1,366,560 days, amounted to 520, or exactly two cycles of the 260 days of the Tzolk'in Calendar. For Cotterell, this was proof enough that the Mayan calendar was not constructed on arbitrarily chosen figures, but built around their knowledge of sunspot activity and its cycles. It offered a further clue as to why Mayan calculations were made over very long periods, enabling them to preview the demise of four previous ages:

> both the Sun's magnetic field and the magnetic field from the sunspots, reversed at around the time the Maya disappeared. The combined

magnetic disturbance led to infertility and genetic mutation on Earth.[105]

He suggests that this is the main reason for the demise of the Mayan civilization during the 9th century.

The 'field effects' on Earth of these extreme changes in the Sun's magnetic field include, for example, the reversal of the direction in which water spins out of a bath plughole or in which a tornado revolves. Cotterell's theory is complex: it takes into account the effect of sunspots on the magnetic field, and the numerical relationships between very long cycles of solar activity, similar to the Mayan 'Five Ages' of the Sun, and the 'magic' super-number.

The problem with such theories is that they endeavour to point too accurately or specifically to particular dates so as to 'coincide' the prophecy with its future fulfilment. Such things as changes in the Sun's or Earth's magnetic field do not happen overnight, and the theory is made implausible by virtue of being based on complicated calculations with huge numbers which are arbitrarily derived and subjectively interpreted. However, it does seem that a change in the Sun's magnetic field, or some similar energy could be one of the consequences of the galactic alignment (see Prophecy 6) projected for the winter solstice of 2012.

For a fuller understanding of the prophecy we need to balance such theories with a modern scientific observation of the Schumann Resonance (SR). This is a low-frequency signal that pulsates between the Earth's electromagnetic field spectrum and the ionosphere. Research indicates that there is a relationship between the Schumann Resonance frequency and human brain waves, and that we are affected by that relationship. It may be thought of as the Earth's heartbeat or pulse. The resonance is due to the space between the surface of the Earth and the conductive properties of the ionosphere which acts as a waveguide. In this cavity, the global electromagnetic resonances are excited by lightning discharges which are, themselves, the source of the resonances. The resonances are currently recorded by many dedicated stations around the world. So far, the SR has held steady, but in recent years monitoring has shown a marked increase from 7.88Hz to 13Hz. The pulsation of low-frequency resonances is not a marker of a threat to the Earth or to life on it. The significance of Schumann Resonance lies in its being one of the most accurate tools used for monitoring climate change and the effects of global warming. More importantly, it is also a tool used to monitor variations in the Earth's magnetic field which is already showing signs of changing; for example, mammals such as dolphins, porpoises and whales use the magnetic poles for navigation purposes, and there is a marked increase in the numbers of beached whales, because their sense of direction is being confused.

A similar pattern has been noted in the number of migratory birds and animals that are discovered away from their traditional routes.

## SUMMARY

The Maya prophesied a recurrence in 2012 of the conditions that may have contributed to the collapse of their civilization in the 9th century. What the prophecy speaks of is excessive sunspot activity, and changes in both the Earth's and Sun's magnetic fields. With the NASA projections for 2012 corroborating this, some form of disaster does seem likely. While the entire Earth may not be threatened, we ought, perhaps, to have contingency plans in place to cope with volcanic eruptions, floods, conflagrations, earthquakes, or a combination of these. Mayan calendars were therefore pointing to 2012 as a date which designates both a series of natural disasters as well as a long and gradual process of environmental change which has already been set in motion.

# PROPHECIES OF EVOLUTION & GENETICS

*The great masters, together with the great spirits, will become a unique being, and they will be able to travel as the wind itself to fall down like the rain does, to heat like the fire does, and most importantly, to impart sacred knowledge.*[106]

## THE MESSAGE

The prophecy, which takes its energy, in part, from the Sage King, Pacal Votan (*see* Prophecy 5) concerns evolutionary changes in human biology that will further develop the mind, the will, and heightened sensitivities, as well as psychic and telepathic powers. Ongoing scientific research appears to confirm these advances.

## COMMENTARY

In this prophecy, we again hear the voice of Pacal Votan, one of the Maya's strongest prophetic voices. The Sage King of the Classical Maya, known as 'Time's Special Witness', speaks of the fascinating concept of humanity's physical biology transforming in conjunction with the calendric cycle of 26,000 years (*see* Prophecy 5). Jenkins also referred to this cycle in terms of our evolution:

> The Maya understood that whereas the 260-day sacred cycle is our period of individual gestation, the 26,000-year cycle is our collective gestation – our collective unfolding as a species. Precession represents a 26,000-year cycle of biological unfolding – a type of spiritual gestation and birth – that Earth and its consciousness-endowed life forms undergo.[107]

Thus, human biology follows its own evolutionary programme in a progression similar to the calendric cycles. We know, of course, that the evolution of living things is a perpetual process and that Dawkins'' *'selfish gene'* continues to dominate its gentler partners so as to ensure only the best survive to be transmitted. The question arises, is evolution only concerned with the body, or does it include the continued development of other aspects of human potential? Pacal Votan was in no doubt that, in the process of continuing evolution, human beings will develop a universal telepathic facility, a considerable heightening of our senses, and a more perfectly focused self-reflective consciousness. These subtler, less obvious, but potentially powerful and world-transforming human faculties have been blunted, even eroded, as we have distanced ourselves from Nature, and put our faith in the materialism and technology that have displaced our instincts and natural abilities. The year 2012 will be marked by the culmination of this 26,000-year 'grand cycle' of evolution. There will be no dramatic, overnight mutations. The prophecy speaks of a time when these more abstract functions will become the subject of the evolutionary process.

Current research shows that the DNA, an element of the genes of every living organism and the chemical memory-bank that stores genetic information is, itself, evolving. An example of this is the continuing evolution of the human brain.[108] A human being is not just a collection of chemicals, but a 'complex electrodynamic being'; as such we are affected by electrodynamic fields both artificial and natural. Richard and Ion Miller found:

> that there is a strong correlation between human behavioural disturbance and geomagnetic field turbulence or isolation from SR frequencies.

[SR: Schumann Resonance. *See* Prophecy 17.] As humans we have extraordinary potentials we have hardly begun to study, much less understand. Creative gifts, intuitions and talents that are unpredictable or emergent may become stabilized in generations to come. Hopefully, we can learn to understand both our emergence from an essentially electromagnetic environment and facilitate our potential for healing, growth and non-local communication.[109]

Such conclusions read like echoes of Pacal Votan's prophecies (*see* Prophecy 5).

Jenkins reminds us that '*the ancient Maya understood something about the nature of the cosmos and the spiritual evolution of humanity that has gone unrecognized in our own world-view*'.[110] The Maya have, indeed, added another level to the concept of evolution, believing that the energy behind it is associated with the kundalini practice we have already noted (*see* Prophecies 4 and 6). D E Rourke' explains that:

Kundalini is the vital force empowering all human growth and development. This crucial life-force is the same as what is known in Hindu cosmology as the serpent power. ... Kundalini is the great evolutionary force, making of each body and

its occupant, a potentially powerful source of
solar wisdom.

This 'secret' evolutionary energy is encoded in the Mayan
mythologies of Kukulcan.

Perhaps the most intriguing aspect of this prophecy
refers to the continued evolution of consciousness, the raw
material of the 'cosmic consciouness' that was the subject
of Prophecy 13. It is this aspect of evolution that forms part
of the message of Shri Mataji Nirmala Devi:

> I am here to tell you about the last breakthrough
> in our evolution. This breakthrough in awareness
> has to happen in these modern times and has
> been, moreover, recorded in the writings of many
> seers.[III]

When the current cycle began, 26,000 years ago,
Neanderthal man was almost extinct and Homo sapiens
were about to take the stage; we can only imagine, and from
artefacts, partially reconstruct the nature of that primitive,
pristine, consciousness. How sensitive was it? Of what, if
anything, was Neanderthal man conscious, beyond the need
to feed, reproduce and survive? Over that period, which is
now rapidly coming to a close, human consciousness has
evolved not only to the point of registering the unlimited

dimensions of the macro and micro cosmos, but more than any other time in history, our consciousness is conscious of itself and the subject of its own research.

### SUMMARY

The prophecy speaks of the natural, evolutionary realization of all aspects of human biological potential, from the genetic content of everyone's DNA to the interrelationship between human electrodynamics and the physical rhythms of the Earth. This interrelationship will, itself, be the context for the further evolution of human consciousness, that is of the brain mechanisms that sustain and operate it, and it will lead the human mind to hitherto unimagined abilities, skills and creativity. Beyond that, since consciousness is the only means we have of relating to God, that is, to the infinite, or the Absolute, its further evolution will lead us to a more mature spirituality. This is a wholly positive prophecy that stands us well in the face of the current and imminent problems we must overcome.

# THE PROPHECY OF TRANSCENDING TECHNOLOGY

*Katun 2 Ahau is the twelfth katun. For half the katun there will be bread; for half the katun there will be water. It is the word of God. Its bread, water and temple are halved. It is the end of the word of God.*[112]

## THE MESSAGE

Katun 2 Ahau will be the first *katun* of the New Age following the winter solstice of 2012. The key to the prophecy is, 'It is the end of the word of God'; what sustains life, physically and spiritually, will be 'halved'. In previous 2 Ahau *katuns*, there have been widespread spiritual and ideological crises and this prophecy warns of another that is imminent. Its likely cause is the undermining of traditionally received spiritual authority by a technology that is displacing our natural human faculties. Thus, the prophecy warns of our need to transcend the all-consuming technocratic culture we have created.

❁

## COMMENTARY

We have already noted that 26,000 years ago, when the current astronomical cycle began, Neanderthal man was at the point of being extinct. His technology amounted to a tool kit of stone implements, scrapers, hand axes and wooden-handled spears, similar to those used by his successors, Homo sapiens. Humanity's 26,000-year journey has produced a technology that, at first, evolved gradually but which, in recent years, has gathered an overwhelming and world-transforming momentum. The prophecy is not just concerned with the nature of change, but with the speed in which it has reduced the world to a global household, and made us observers of both the microscopic finite and the telescopic infinite. In this process, technology has failed to meet the conditions that would ensure our survival and that of the planet.

Moore's Law, first applied to the exponential increase of computer components, suggests that the rate of technological change will soon be close to being infinite, taking us towards a new concept called 'Singularity'. The Singularity Watch defines the concept as *'the rise of super intelligent life, created through the improvement of human tools by the acceleration of technological progress reaching the point of infinity'*.[113] The end product, however, is already with us in the form of 'spiritual machines', robotics, and artificial intelligence that aims to be an organic extension of ourselves.[114] Kubrick's *2001: A Space Odyssey*, famously told of the spacecraft computer, HAL, that had a mind of its own. This raises the somewhat threatening but critical question as to whether machines can attain consciousness. The Dalai Lama' is on record as saying:

> I can't totally rule out the possibility that, if all the external conditions and the karmic action were there, a stream of consciousness might actually

enter into a computer. There is a possibility that a
scientist who has very much involved his whole life
[with computers], then, in the next life he would
be reborn in a computer! [laughter] Then this
machine, which is half-human and half-machine,
has been reincarnated. I feel this question about
computers will be resolved only by time. We just
have to wait and see ...until it actually happens.[115]

The prophecy warns that we have not begun to address the
relationship between technology and spirituality. The
scientist and ecologist, Dr Charles Birch has warned that,:

Our technological civilization has not adapted to
the needs of survival ... There is something
radically wrong with the way we are living on
Earth today. The sort of society we are building
with the aid of science and technology has self-
destructive features built into it.[116]

The prophecy implies that the proper response is for us to
transcend this technology. It is helpful and encouraging to
bear in mind that the root meaning of the Greek, *techne,*
was also used of the techniques of the artist, and that the
philosopher, Heidegger,[117] poignantly reminded us that
there was '*once a time when the bringing-forth of the true into the*

*beautiful was also called the* techne'. Pinchbeck's* suggestion is important:

> if art contains a saving power, it is not in the
> atomized artworks produced by individual
> subjects, but in a deeper collective vision that sees
> the world as a work of art.

It seems, then, that the most effective way for humanity to transcend technology, and redress the problems with which it confronts us, is by creative living. A further implication of the prophecy is that we are perfectly capable of controlling our runaway technology, since *'we ourselves ... are the best and most sophisticated technology there is – we are the path beyond technology'*.[118]

## SUMMARY

The prophecy indicates that the consequences of hypertechnology are far-reaching. It has exceeded the point where it serves humanity in securing a better quality of life; it has accelerated the extent to which we have given ourselves over to materialistic and consumerist values; it has contributed to our severance from Nature and 'natural time' (*see* Prophecy 20). The prophecy returns us to the running theme of our need to recover our natural integration and experience of unity with Nature (*see* Prophecy 16). The prophecy speaks of humanity's urgent need to transcend a technology that is rapidly approaching the point where the technology will transcend humanity.

# THE PROPHECY
# OF TIME

*A time will come when the katun-folds*
*will have passed away, when they will be found*
*no longer, because the count of tuns is*
*reunited.*

**Chilam Balam of Tizimin** [119]

The prophecy of the reuniting of the count of *tuns* tells us that time will no longer be divided into ongoing periods. The prophecy speaks of the radical change of consciousness that must take place if humanity is to understand that time is cyclic and not linear. Time understood as cyclic means that the prophecy of the 2012 galactic synchronization (*see* Prophecy 6) also speaks of a new dimensional time stream the Maya plotted in their calendars. The prophecy addresses the problem of the artificiality of the Gregorian calendar which imposes a time structure that is out of tune with time's natural cycles.

❖

## COMMENTARY

The prophecy is about time itself, and it brings us to the very centre of the Mayan message, that time is cyclic and not linear. As José Argüelles assures us:

> we have the opportunity to shift one of our core
> beliefs, the belief that time is linear. It is the 12
> Moon calendar that holds in place the belief in the

past, present and future. Time is a cycle, not a line.
Each time the cycle turns we have the opportunity
to make our lives better.[120]

Fritjof Capra draws our attention to the extent to which
there are parallels and interconnections between modern
physics, Eastern mysticism and perceptions of mysticism
generally.

Thus, the awareness of the profound harmony
between the world-view of modern physics and the
views of Eastern mysticism now appears as an
integral part of a much larger cultural
transformation, leading to the emergence of a new
vision of reality that will require a fundamental
change in our thoughts, perceptions and values.[121]

This 'larger cultural transformation' can well be extended to
include Mayan mysticism and cosmology. To understand
the significance of this prophecy, it is necessary for the
Western mind to let go of its linear concept of time. For the
purpose of documenting history, and for planning current
and future events, it is conventionally useful to *record* time
in a linear format, but the Mayan concept is that time itself
is cyclic, or because of imbrication and overlaps, spiral. As
we have seen, it is the repetition of the characteristics of

cycles of time that enabled the Maya to prophesy the recurrence of events.

Probably the most extraordinary feature of the Mayan calendars is their perception of the interrelationship of time and space. Our own understanding of time and space has been conditioned by the world-views of Newton and Descartes, which have contributed so much to the radical dualism characteristic of Western culture. Our mindset is conditioned to make distinctions between spirit and matter, mind and matter, space and time, until, that is, Einstein, and subsequently modern physics, radically revised these concepts.

The Maya, as if in anticipation of the non-duality of everything, understood mythology to be concrete, that the gods represented the energies and laws of nature, and that everything was held together by a single intelligent energy they named Hunab Ku, the 'Giver of Movement and Measure'. The path of dualism followed by Western philosophy has led us to a crisis of identity, a spiritual schizophrenia, and the sense of being caught between the wood and the bark of fundamental oppositions. The Maya, following their instinctual sense of a unifying intelligent energy, have lived with the cyclic laws that hold everything in balance. Space-time is the framework of this unity and balance, an abstraction made concrete in their calendars.

The prophecy speaks of the radical change in consciousness that must take place if we are to experience this interrelatedness, and the cyclic or spiral nature of time. We will have to let go of the concept of time as 'duration', that it is not a fixed value or measure, but something that is fluid and malleable. This perception has always been shared by mystics of all religions. The 13th-century Zen master, Dogen Zenji, explained that:

> the idea of passing may be called time, but it is an incorrect idea, for since one sees it only as passing one cannot understand that it stays just where it is.

Pinchbeck comes to a similar conclusion:

> The existence of a four-dimensional space-time continuum means that what we perceive as the linear direction of time is only an illusion created by our particular perspective.[122]

The prophecy of time thus becomes one of a new dimensional time stream which was plotted by the Maya in their calendars. The change in the perception of time calls us to experience the timelessness of the present moment.

The Julian and Gregorian calendars have imposed an arbitrary time structure which is out of harmony with the cycles of nature. The prophecy implies that not only will we become actively conscious of the natural cycles, but that in so doing, we will recover time's integration with nature and its cosmic energies. To achieve this, Argüelles has proposed the very plausible idea of changing our 12-moon calendar to a 13-moon calendar which he suggests is an entirely natural time rhythm. He argues that:

> The simple and easiest way to reprogram your daily awareness of the actual nature of time is to follow the 13-Moon calendar ... For every one time we go round the Sun, the Moon goes round the Earth 13 times. The year has already been divided by nature.[123]

Implementing this suggestion of changing to the 13-Moon calendar might well be one of the ways the prophecy could be fulfilled. In effect, what Argüelles calls 'Dreamspell' is a system of time-keeping that applies the ancient Mayan time-science to our own culture.

> Like the Maya who preceded us, we shall understand that the path to the stars is through the senses and that a proper utilization of our mind as the auto-regulatory control factor will help facilitate the passage to different levels or dimensions of being.[124]

A glance at Appendix 3 will show how the Tzolk'in and the Haab calendars lock into each other. This intermeshing can also be thought of as an imbrication, or the overlapping of two different ways of indicating a specific moment in time; that moment will 'happen' differently according to the calendar used, but in sync if the calendars are used together. The idea of periods of time overlapping is not one that our Western mind finds easy to grasp, but the concept works well with the idea of 'natural time' of Earth being in harmony with the cycles of the Moon and Sun. Imbrication is well illustrated by the overlapping lines of a spiral. A past event on the spiral will be 'echoed' at the 'future' corresponding points of the spiral as a sign of what has past; a future event will be 'shadowed' on the spiral's present moment; a present event through successive 'present' moments is the actualization of both the past and the future. The various systems of 'keeping' time are therefore not necessarily conscious of the 'same' time, but of different moments *in* time experienced simultaneously. Barbara Tedlock came to the same conclusion about the Mayan consciousness of time.

> It appears that Mayan peoples once had differing systems of timekeeping for separate areas of their biological, astrological, religious, and social realities, and that these systems underwent a process of totalization within the overlapping, intermeshing cycles of their calendars.[125]

## SUMMARY

The prophecy speaks of our need to change our core belief
about the nature of time. The year 2012 implies that we have
the opportunity to shift our understanding of what time
is, and how it functions. The prophecy heightens the
problems caused by our current notion of time as linear
which, through the Julian and Gregorian calendars, has
conditioned the way we think about time. The prophecy is
saying that what 2012 marks, is not the end of time in the
sense of it being the end of the world, but the end of the
conventional way we understand and experience time.

> We have thus come to comprehend that our
> notions of a three-dimensional Euclidean space
> and of linear flowing time are limited to our
> ordinary experience of the physical world and have
> to be completely abandoned when we extend this
> experience.[126]

By this abandonment, we shall acquire a deeper understanding and, by consequence, a deeper experience. Our
awareness of these principles will gather considerable
momentum towards 2012, but to change from a concept of
time as linear, to that of it being cyclic, will require a huge
leap in our perception.

# THE PROPHECY THAT WE ARE THE PROPHECY

*This is the record of the wisdom of the book in which is set down the course of each katun ... whether it is good or bad. These things shall be accomplished. No one shall cause them to cease.*

The Book of Chilam Balam of Chumayel [127]

The prophecies for 2012 point, inevitably, to the responsibility of those who would live during and beyond the period of the final katun of this age. They make it clear, that only by the individual and collective choices we now make can we avert the disaster facing our planet and human civilization. We have the technology, we have the science, but despite our sophisticated civilization, we are spiritually immature, and it remains to be seen if we can be sufficiently determined to act on the priorities facing us.

## COMMENTARY

The prophecy confronts us with the sum of the prophetic messages – our inescapable responsibility of accepting that we are the 'Time'. we are the *living* prophecy of which all the prophecies speak. From 13 August 3114 BCE, the start-date of the Long Count Calendar, the *baktuns* have cycled to terminate on 21 December 2012. We are now living through the last 5 years of the 5,125-year Long Count, or Creation Cycle, which are also the final years of the 26,000-year Great Cycle, the precession of the equinoxes, and galactic synchronization. We have not chosen to live our lives at this time, we have had 'greatness thrust upon' us. We are living through a period of radical transformation; we are witnesses to the passing of an old World, or Sun, and to the birth of its successor. Since the extinction of Neanderthal man 26,000 years ago, our period is, in all its aspects of history, politics, demography, climate, ecology, astronomy, technology, consciousness and astrology, unprecedented in human history. The prophecy calls us not to be spectators, but to be engaged in the processes of change.

The prophecy is positive, it tells us that we have a 'window of opportunity', and that by the choices we make we can determine a creative future for our civilization and our planet. It is a matter of the way we form our conscious relationships with each other, with Nature, with the totality of the biosphere. Other prophecies have indicated that this period of transition towards and following 2012, will not be easy. Life on Earth, in terms of evolution, is a learning curve for everything that lives, requiring constant adjustment and adaptation. One of the possible outcomes we have considered is the destruction of the planet as a result of natural disaster, environmental degradation, or both. In this event, what subsequently 'happens' to individuals is dependent of their world-view, on whether they believe in some form of life after death, a continuum, conscious or otherwise. If death is understood as an absolute termination of life in any form, then the manner of dying will dominate. The death of the Earth, however, is unlikely; life will almost certainly continue beyond 2012, and what will determine the quality of that life falls on present generations to decide.

> We are living in what the Greeks called the *kairos* – the right moment – for 'metamorphosis of the gods', of the fundamental principles and symbols. ... Coming generations will have to take account of this momentous transformation if humanity is not to destroy itself through the might of its own technology and science ... So much is at stake and so much depends on the psychological constitution of the modern man.[128]

Crisis, be it war, plague or a threat to the planet, has a way of bringing people together. The crisis we are facing gives us a very special, and urgent, opportunity to realize unity, both among ourselves and as 'a planetary organism in contact with itself anywhere on the planet'. Only by concentrating on our own breath will we be able to take the one breath together.

## SUMMARY

The prophecy confronts us with the question, knowing that we are the prophecy, what does it mean to be nearing the completion of the precession of the equinoxes, and what can we expect, personally as well as planetarily, in 2012? The truth is, we can have no expectation, we do not know what will happen. Prophecies speak of our potential for personal divinity; they speak of the transformation of our consciousness; they speak of the evolutionary potential of human senses and faculties, as yet barely developed; they speak of a recovered sense of oneness with Nature in its universal totality. Most importantly, the prophecy points to us as the agents for necessary and radical change. We cannot pass the buck.

# 2012:
# SUMMARY &
# CONCLUSIONS

*The prophecies declared it to the people*
*on that day ... As trees grow in the land, ...*
*our prophecies will prove true. These are the*
*words that must be spoken: The prophecies*
*are a solemn trust from the ancient time.*
*They are the first news of event, and a*
*valuable warning of things to come.*

Chilam Balam of Tizimin

In the tradition of true prophecy, the Maya are warning us of what will happen to our civilization if we simply continue as we are now. What, then, are the principal themes of the prophecies we need, urgently, to consider?

## THE CALENDAR END DATE

The winter solstice of 21 December 2012 terminates both the Mayan Long Count Calendar and the 26,000-year period of precession (*see* Prophecy 6). In terms of astronomy this will be apparent in a conjunction of planets, referred to as 'galactic synchronization'. The six months, from the transit of Venus on 6 June 2012 to 21 December 2012, will see the gradual alignment of an extraordinary conjunction that last occurred 26,000 years ago. It can be summarized thus:

i) The Sun will be at the exact centre of the galaxy. For the Maya, this centre, or 'Dark Rift', is symbolic of the womb, the entrance to the underworld, death and regeneration.

ii) The conjunction includes Pluto, Jupiter, Saturn and Neptune.

iii) Pluto is the planet of radical transformation, death and rebirth. Saturn the planet of difficult learning experiences. Jupiter is the planet of expansion, focusing the strong energies of the other planets involved. Jupiter appears to be the focus of energies that suggest changes in religious belief and philosophical systems. Neptune's critical contribution also points to spirituality, but in addition, to confusion and flooding.

The combined energies of these planetary tendencies both form the context and set the general trend for the prophecies. The dominant 'message' of galactic synchronization would seem to be that humanity will face radical and threatening change, but with a positive potential (*see* Prophecies 5, 12, 13, 15 and 16); it will have to face a challenging learning curve, the abandonment of some old concepts, and a positive response to new perceptions; it will have the chance to develop spiritually and psychically, but will also see an escalation of international tension and conflict against the background of increasing ecological problems. The cosmic balance of the conjunction suggests that humanity will mature spiritually, but that the transition through 2012 and beyond will be problematic.

## GLOBAL CATASTROPHE

The end of life on the planet, and the possible destruction of the planet itself, is a familiar theme that has appeared regularly throughout history, carried to us by 'false messiahs'. Warning of our imminent demise reappears from time to time in the form of millennial cults, and passionate individuals who distribute tracts and pace the pavements with an 'End of the World' placard in hand. Such terminal global catastrophe is also one of the most persistent interpretations of the Mayan prophecies pointing to 2012, presumably because it is the most radical, dramatic and newsworthy. This apocalyptic reading of the prophecy has its roots in the Mayan mythology of the Five Ages, or Suns (*see* Prophecies 1 and 15). Each period of the Five Suns has ended with global catastrophe and the prophecy of a recurrence is built into the approaching end of the current age, it being the Fifth Sun. Never sure the Sun would rise again, there is a suggestion in Mayan mythology that they were afraid of the Sun, and that human sacrifice was a way of appeasing it. They lived with the anxiety that one day the Sun's life-giving force would no longer nourish the Earth and that the last age of the Sun would also be the last age of mankind.

This is not, however, an interpretation encouraged by contemporary Mayan elders, who are concerned, even angered, by Western misuse of the sources. What they endeavour to make us understand is that while we are, indeed, approaching the end of a World Age, we live on the cusp of a new age; this will be a period of transition, a cosmic rite of passage, a genesis which, while confronting us with problems of radical adjustment, offers all the potential embodied in the concept of birth, rebirth and new life (*see* Prophecies, 12, 18, 19 and 20)

## EARTH CHANGES

Prophecy 17 speaks of changes in the Earth's magnetic field. This is linked to extreme activity on the Sun. The consequences of alterations to the Sun's magnetic field, and the unprecedented increase in sunspot activity, with similar radical shifts in the Earth's poles are, themselves, pointers to an 'End of Age' scenario. It remains a mystery how the Maya, or any other ancient civilization had access, as naked-eye 'sky-watchers', to information about sunspot activity, but they seem not only to have known about sunspots but also that they affected human life and the Earth's magnetic fields. The Earth's adjustment to fluctuations of the Sun's activity results in physical changes to the structure of the Earth in terms, for example, of continental drift and the melting and movement of the icecaps. The Mayan prophecy indicates that the next sequence of violent sunspot activity will take place in 2012, with possible radical consequences for the Earth. This is corroborated by NASA (*see* Prophecy 17 and Science@NASA.gov). Some of the data the Maya accumulated for sunspot activity in relation to its effect on Earth, was recorded in hieroglyphs on the famous Lid of

Palenque, the cover sealing the sarcophagus of the Mayan King, Pacal Votan (*see* Prophecy 5). The Maya's deliberate deformation of the skull at birth to produce a simian effect (*see* Introduction) may have caused changes to the brain that enhanced their mental ability to cope with the vast mathematical calculations involved.

The main thrust of this prophecy draws on the latent potential of the brain to form an energy-related and consciousness-related connection to changes in the Earth's magnetic fields. It is, in part, an answer to the mystery as to how the Maya acquired their knowledge of mathematics and astronomy; Argüelles refers to our ability '*to direct and receive galactic information from different levels of the universal electromagnetic ocean*';[129] the Russian scientist, Kozyrev [130] spoke of a magnetic field activity that brings the human being '*into an almost direct interaction with cosmic energy-information flows*', enabling us '*to see and study in detail the Maya information flow which reached our planet nearly three thousand years ago*'. Thus, the prophecy, while alarmist in terms of Earth changes, is positive in terms of humanity acquiring new means of accessing knowledge. What it points to are new, 'evolutionary' developments of human faculties (*see below* and Prophecy 18).

The implication of the prophecy of Earth changes for ecology (*see* Prophecy 16) are, inevitably, the clearest and most apparent. We have no need to dwell on what we daily confront in the media about global warming, the precarious state of the Earth's biosphere, the threat to the Earth's base resonance frequency, the relationship between biosphere and noosphere. This aspect of the prophecy points us to our relationship with nature, that if we are to survive we need to understand 'Nature' in all of its manifestations, in terms of partnership rather than exploitation.

The potential contained in this prophecy is hugely exciting for humanity because it concerns our need to reform our self-identity. The prophecy calls us to reconsider what it means to be a human being in the broader context of the whole of Nature, to rethink our relationship with it, and to acquire a new understanding of the meaning and purpose of life. The biblical religions speak of our need of redemption, of atonement, that is of our need for 'at-one-ment' with God, and the energies of cosmic life. Eastern religions speak of the need to transcend duality through enlightenment and absorption. The Mayan prophecy challenges us to begin where we are, to look at our immediate surroundings, and to recover the sense, once held by ancestors we call 'primitive', of being an integral part of everything. The prophecy tells us that by setting out to reintegrate with Nature, we shall, ourselves, be regenerated.

It is encouraging that already there are positive far-reaching responses to the problems of the planet, such as

Lovelock's Gaia initiative,[131] and programmes in schools and universities such as the Environmental Education and Urban Ecology Initiatives.

## SCIENCE AND TECHNOLOGY

The Maya are renowned for their innovative agriculture, their monumental architecture, gold and copper work, hieroglyphic writing, and for the mathematics and astronomy represented by their calendars (*see* Appendices).

The Maya had also developed an 'inner' technology that enabled them to apply their knowledge of mathematics to astronomy, not just to the point of collecting and recording data, but of enabling them to understand their world, their place in it, who they were, and the purpose of life. It is of this inner technology that Prophecy 19 speaks. Our own technology has overtaken us, it is almost beyond our control, and the hypersophisticated technology of modern warfare puts the human race and the planet at risk.

Electronic communication, cell phones, WiFi, satellite navigation and telemetry, computers, pocket PCs and organizers, email and the internet, etc. put an entire virtual world and its population into our hands. The state-of-the-art technology has a life of little more than a day, the speed of change far beyond our capacity to adapt and comprehend.

Undoubtedly, the Maya had faculties we lack, or perhaps skills we have lost because we have invented a technology that displaces them. Their mathematical ability without the aid of even an abacus, their knowledge of astronomy, their ability to deal with huge numbers and vast cycles of time, implies a facility that we associate with computers. We have given our minds over to the technology it has invented. It is generally accepted that we have never developed the genetic potential with which we are born; Prophecy 18 speaks of a continued evolution that will develop and heighten our intuition and psychic ability; it speaks of the possibility that we may be able to communicate with someone at a great distance without the use of any mechanical device.

By our ability to isolate genes and the DNA, we can now determine the life form of living things, selecting the sex, intelligence, physical stature and appearance, by genetic modification. In parallel we can do all of this artificially by constructing robots that will do absolutely everything for us. Our technology has outgrown our maturity to control it, and if it outgrows our will to control it, we may well be replaced by it. The Dalai Lama allows for the possibility that '*a stream of consciousness might actually enter into a computer*' (*see* Prophecy 19). The implication is that a scientist might, one day, be reincarnated as a laptop.

The attraction of the ecological, organic 'good life', the

'return to nature', the yearning for simplicity, are reactions to the complexities of our high-tech culture. Argüelles' has plausibly argued that our sense of time is artificial because throughout history our lives have been framed by a calendar that is out of sync with 'natural time' (*see* Prophecy 20). He suggests that we adopt the 13-moon calendar, the clock that nature has given us and which we ignore at great cost. Implicit in prophecies that speak of science and technology is our need to change from a linear to a cyclic notion of time. Remaining locked into a concept of time as duration is merely convenient, it is useful for keeping records and planning future events, but it also imposes finitude, a sense of termination, of history as something past and finished, and it inhibits the creative, liberating sense of the continuum characteristic of the cyclic concept of time.

## UNITY AND ENLIGHTENED TEACHERS

Early in the 20th century we began to experience the world as a global village; at the beginning the 21st century the world has become a global household. Despite this proximity, humanity has not yet realized its oneness, its unitary nature as a single planetary organism. The year 2012 signals the pivotal moment when humanity will undergo a radical change. Through some profound mind- and soul-altering event, it will experience an evolutionary shift from atomized, individual human consciousness to that of a unified organism that breaths, moves and works together. The breaking down of the various barriers that divide people is a strikingly optimistic prophecy in face of established and growing fundamentalist entrenchments. Despite this, there are both secular and religious initiatives working to overcome the traditional differences. They do not always meet with success. *The Times* of 10 May 2007 reported one of the Archbishop of Canterbury's interfaith conferences, 'Building Bridges' was frustrated by having the Muslim-Christian dialogue conference refused by the Malaysian Government. Dr Rowan Williams warned of *'the terrible consequences'* of fear caused by division.

> We must keep our bridges in good repair, the bridges for listening and sympathy, hearing the truth from one another, learning what the other experience is like.[132]

What the prophecy of unity calls for (*see* Prophecy 11) is an unprecedented unity of purpose cutting across language, culture and belief, a 'harmonic convergence' of the spiritually adept of all faiths and traditions. It is from this group of spiritually mature people that we must look for leadership. The prophecy reminds us of our need of gifted teachers (*see* Prophecy 2) who will encourage increasing numbers to take up a practice of meditation, the means of harmonizing our individual and collective psychic and conscious rhythms in the form of a one-pointed focus. In the context of Buddhist meditation, temporal space-experience,

> is converted into a simultaneous coexistence, the side-by-side existence of things ... and this again does not remain static but becomes a living continuum in which time and space are integrated.[133]

Between now and 2012, such spiritually minded people, representing every living faith, are together capable of creating a type of spiritual battery to charge the human mental environment so as to turn errant humanity from its present course.

## WE ARE THE PROPHECY

Although the prophecies speak of a cosmic shift in consciousness and evolutionary potential, we have to engage the processes ourselves, it is not merely a question of passively waiting for it to happen. What is about to occur depends entirely on how we respond to the Mayan prophecies for 2012. This is why we also speak of spiritual mastery. There are at least as many spiritual masters on the planet today as there are armed terrorists, and certainly there are as many people on this Earth who have attained sufficient spiritual mastery as to exceed the number of humans actively enlisted in the world's armies.

The German philosopher, Karl Jaspers, coined the term 'Axial Age' to describe the period 800 BCE–200 CE, as having been formative for all future philosophy and religion. He argued that during this period, similar energies in the Occident, India and China, laid down the spiritual foundations on which humanity continues to rest today.[134] These energies were drawn from many sources, for example, from the monotheism of the Old Testament and its prophetic message, the Buddha, Confucius, the Upanishads, Zoroaster, and Socrates. Jaspers' thesis has been expanded to suggest that there have been other Axial Ages, such as the Renaissance, the Enlightenment, and the Age of Reason. These different periods have characteristics in common, such as, a quest for meaning and the purpose of life, the emergence of new religious thinkers and leaders, and prevailing sociopolitical conditions. These characteristics resonate with the Mayan prophecies directed to our own Age and its conclusion in 2012, specifically those referring to new teachers and masters (Prophecy 2), and our quest for knowledge and meaning (Prophecies 12 and 13). What is of equal significance is that the original Axial Age designated by Jaspers was characterized by the powerful triple conjunction of Uranus, Neptune and Pluto.

> Astronomically, this was the only era in recorded history [590–550 BCE] in which the Uranus-Neptune cycle, the Uranus-Pluto cycle, and the Neptune-Pluto cycle coincided in such a close triple conjunction ... the coinciding historical and cultural phenomena seem to have formed an enormous archetypal wave ...[135]

The Maya prophesied that we, together with the precession of the equinoxes, would come full circle. The hugely significant galactic synchronization of 2012 (*see* Prophecy 6) is the context of the spiritual and cultural renewal that will enable us to solve our ecological problems and usher in a new Axial Age. The dominant message emerging from the Mayan prophecies for 2012 is that we are the prophecy, and that whatever happens in the future is dependent on the choices we make.

# APPENDICES:
# THE CALENDARS

*Time became a more personal concept, relative
to the observer who measures it.*

Stephen Hawking

*What is time? It is a secret – lacking in
substance and yet almighty.*

Thomas Mann, *The Magic Mountain*

*Calendars were, and still are, used by the Maya
to map and structure various aspects of human
experience, from agricultural activities to
observed cycles in the sky. ... Long ago they
intuited that the celestial cycles harmoniously
reflect cycles on Earth.*

John Major Jenkins

# APPENDIX I

# THE TUN

*The glyph for the Tun*

The Tun year is made up of 18 months, each of 20 days, giving a period of 360 days. The remaining 5-day period is called the Wayeb, a time when the gods withdraw their support from humanity. The full 365-day period, is called the Haab. The Tun has probably been in use since the 6th century BCE, its start-date being the December winter solstice.

*The 360-day period was considered among the Maya as a time of prophecy. ... The Tun became the basic unit of the prophetic calendars of the Maya.*

**Calleman**

The calendric system most approximating the Gregorian calendar is called the Tun. With a 360-day year, it is the equivalent of our own 365-day calendar of the solar year, and was developed by pre-Columbian Mesoamerican cultures many centuries before the calendar introduced by Julius Caesar in 46 BCE. It was this, the Julian calendar, that was modified by an Italian doctor and chronologist, Aloysius Lilius; these alterations were officially adopted by a decree of Pope Gregory XIII on the 24 February 1582.

However, there are clear differences between the Tun and the Gregorian calendar. The Tun is built around eighteen 20-day months which provides a year of 360 days to which was added a final, brief, 5-day period. This 365-day cycle, the Haab, may be thought of as a civil or secular calendar, simply a physical account of the Earth's passage round the Sun, used for noting the turning of the seasons and thus, for agriculture, for planning the planting and harvesting of crops. The Tun, in contrast, may be read as a spiritual cycle. Not only does it append the extra 5 intercalated days, but it endows them with deep religious significance.

Furthermore, the Tun takes no account of the missing quarter days for which the Gregorian calendar compensates with the 'leap' year registered every four years by adding a 29th day to February. For this reason the Tun is sometimes called the 'Vague Year'. There is a tradition that suggests the Maya made up these quarter days every

52 years when 13 'leap' days are added.

During the final intercalated 5-day month of the Haab year, known as the Wayeb, meaning 'nameless', the gods were believed to be absent, or resting. Their withdrawal meant the Maya could not rely on their support. Short as it was, it was a period of fear and darkness, a time fraught with danger and death, and observed by prayer and mourning. During the Wayeb, fires were extinguished and people had to eat cold food. It was not an auspicious time to get married and a person unlucky enough to be born during the Wayeb was expected to have a difficult and unhappy life.

The following table shows that each of the 20 days of the month carried a name, a number, a glyph, and a meaning or association.

# TABLE 1: THE DAY NAMES

| YUCATEC DAY NAME | DAY NUMBER | GLYPH | MEANING OR ASSOCIATION |
|---|---|---|---|
| Imix | 1 | | World, water lily. Alligator and the reptilian body of the planet Earth, or the world. |
| Ik | 2 | | Air, wind, breath, and life. Also, violence. |
| Ak'b'al | 3 | | 'Night-House' or darkness, the underworld. Also, evil. |
| K'an | 4 | | Maize, seed, sign of the young Maize Lord who brings abundance, ripeness. Also lizard, net. |
| Chikchan | 5 | | Snake, the celestial serpent. |
| Kimi | 6 | | Death |
| Manik | 7 | | Deer, sign of the Lord of the hunt. Also, hand. |

| | | | |
|---|---|---|---|
| Lamat | 8 | | Rabbit, sign of the planet Venus. Also, sunset. |
| Muluc | 9 | | Water, symbolized by jade. An aspect of the water deities. Also, rain and fish. |
| Ok | 10 | | Dog, the Sun's guide through the underworld. |
| Chuwen | 11 | | Monkey, the great craftsman, patron of the arts and knowledge. Also, thread. |
| Eb | 12 | | Grass, or point, associated with rain and storms. Also, tooth and road. |
| B'en | 13 | | Reed – which fosters the growth of corn, cane, and man. |
| Ix | 14 | | Jaguar – the night Sun. Also, maize. |
| Men | 15 | | Eagle, the wise one, bird and Moon. |
| Ki'b | 16 | | Vulture, owl – death-birds of night and day. Also, soul, wax and insect. |

| | | | |
|---|---|---|---|
| Kab'an | 17 | | Earthquake, thus formidable power. Also, season, Earth, thought. |
| Etz'nab | 18 | | Knife, flint, the obsidian sacrificial blade. |
| Kawac | 19 | | Storm or rain – the celestial dragon, serpents, gods of thunder and lightning. |
| Ahau | 20 | | Lord, the radiant Sun god. Also, light. |

In the same way, each of the 18 months, or *winals*, of the 365-day Haab year were given a name, a number, a glyph, and a meaning or association.

## TABLE 2: THE MONTHS OF THE HAAB YEAR

| MONTH NAME | MONTH NUMBER | GLYPH | MEANING OR ASSOCIATION |
|---|---|---|---|
| Pop | 1 | | Mat Resurrection |
| Wo | 2 | | Frog Departure of the waters Black conjunction |

| Sip | 3 |  | Stag<br>Slaughter of dogs<br>Red conjunction |
| Sots | 4 | | Bat<br>Little vigil |
| Sek | 5 | | Skull<br>Grand vigil |
| Xul | 6 | | End<br>Dog<br>Dry things |
| Yaxk'in | 7 | | Tender, new, green Sun<br>Meal of corn and beans |
| Mol | 8 |  | Reunion<br>Little feast of Lords<br>Water |
| Ch'en | 9 | | Well<br>Black storm<br>Grand feast of Lords |
| Yax | 10 | | Little feast of the dead<br>Green storm |
| Sak | 11 |  | Grand feast of the dead<br>White storm |
| Keh | 12 |  | Deer<br>Sweeping<br>Red storm |

| | | | |
|---|---|---|---|
| Mak | 13 | | Enclosed<br>Cover<br>Small hay |
| K'ank'in | 14 | | Mature, yellow Sun<br>Large hay |
| Muwan | 15 | | Owl<br>Flamingo |
| Pax | 16 | | Music<br>Planting time<br>Raising of the banners |
| K'ayab | 17 | | Turtle<br>Lowering of the water |
| Kumk'u | 18 | | Dark god<br>Granary<br>Shrinking |
| Wayeb | The 5 days | | Spectres<br>Empty days<br>Unlucky days |

In the post-Classical period the 20 days of the months were numbered 1-19, but during the Classical period, c.300–c.1900 CE, the last day of a month was regarded as the 'seating' or *chum*, or day '0' of the following month. Thus, for example, the last day of the 14th month, K'ank'in, would have been written down as *chum* Muwan, which was taken as the first day of Muwan, or '0' Muwan, known also as the 'seating' of Muwan, with the following day being the 1st of Muwan, and so on to the 20th. The first day of the New Year would therefore be '0' Pop, followed by 1 Pop, 2 Pop etc. Otherwise, the combination of date and name of the month runs on the same pattern as the months of the Gregorian calendar, for example, Thursday 1st, Friday 2nd, Saturday 3rd, etc. of March.

From approximately the time of the post-Classical Spanish conquest of the Yucatan, which started early in the 16th century, the first day of Pop was numbered 1 instead of 0, thus the year began 1 Pop and ended 5 Wayeb. The probable reason for anticipating the new month by the *chum*, is suggested by the Mayan belief that the influence of any given time span is sensed *before* it begins, and lingers *beyond* its actual, dated end. Thus the Mayan philosophy of time is superimposed over the methods of recording time.

# APPENDIX 2

# THE TZOLK'IN

The Tzolk'in calendar is made up of a 20-day week cycled 13 times, to give a period of 260 days. This is a sacred count of days, not simply a short year, but a fixed period in its own right with its own significance. When the 260-day cycle is completed, it begins again.

*The Tzolk'in is still regarded as the Sacred Calendar among the Maya, reflecting a process of divine creation that proceeds without interruption.*

### Calleman

The Yucatec word *'tzolk'in'* means 'count of days', and was the calendar most used by the Maya, who continue to use it today in the Yucatan, Guatemala, Belize and Honduras. It is sometimes referred to as the 'Sacred Cycle' in contrast to the secular cycle of the 365-day Haab. The basic unit of the Tzolk'in is a sequence of 20 days, which may be thought of as a 20-day week, which is cycled 13 times. Thus, the first 13 of the 20 days are numbered as such, 1–13, with the 14th day numbered again as '1', the 15th as '2', and so on. The names of the days and their glyphs are, of course, the same as for those of the days for the Tun month. For the Tzolk'in, however, their dominating significance is associated with agriculture and the cycle of creation.

# TABLE 3: TZOLK'IN OR SACRED DAY CALENDAR CYCLE

| 20 YUCATEC DAY NAMES | 1–13 CYCLE | CROP GROWTH ETC. DURING 13-DAY CYCLE |
|---|---|---|
| 1. Imix | 1 | Sowing |
| 2. Ik | 2 | |
| 3. Ak'b'al | 3 | Germination |
| 4. K'an | 4 | |
| 5. Chikchan | 5 | Sprouting |
| 6. Kimi | 6 | |
| 7. Manik | 7 | Development |
| 8. Lamat | 8 | |
| 9. Muluc | 9 | Budding |
| 10. Ok | 10 | |
| 11. Chuwen | 11 | Flowering |
| 12. Eb | 12 | |
| 13. B'en | 13 | Fruition |
| 14. Ix | 1 | |
| 15. Men | 2 | |
| 16. K'ib | 3 | |
| 17. Kab'an | 4 | |
| 18. Etz'nab | 5 | |
| 19. Kawac | 6 | |
| 20. Ahau | 7 | |
| 1. Imix | | |
| Etc. | 8 | Sowing |
| Etc. | Etc. | Etc. |

For any given day to recur on the same number, a cycle of 260 days is required. Once the full cycle is completed, it is repeated. As the crop sowing and growth indicators show, the calendar was used to organize agriculture as well as to plan family events, such as marriages, to mark religious and ceremonial occasions, and for divination.

Many theories endeavour to account for the significance of the numbers 13 and 20. Both are important, even sacred, numbers which have multilayered mythological readings. The number 13 carried deep esoteric significance with Chac, the patron god of 13, being also the god of rain and fertility, and to this must be added the symbolism associated with the 13 Heavens and Upper Levels of Mayan mythology. Longhena [136] explains that 20 was a key number in the vigesimal system, and was represented in the codices by the Moon glyph. Unsurprisingly, then, the Maya registered the course of time in 20-year cycles, the *katun*, and in multiples of this amounting, approximately, to 400-year blocks of time, known as the *baktun*. The more mundane and practical explanation is that '20' as the base-number in the system of counting (*see* Introduction) was drawn simply from the number of fingers and toes, and that 20 x 13 gives us the 260 days, significantly the period required for mountain maize, the Maya's staple crop, to grow and ripen, or roughly the 9 months associated with the period of human gestation. Jenkins makes the intriguing suggestion

that the 260-day Tzolk'in cycle is a numerical shadow of
the cycle of precession (*see* Prophecy 6), and that this also
'*represents a 26,000-year cycle of biological unfolding – a type of
spiritual gestation and birth – that Earth and its consciousness-
endowed life-forms undergo*'.[137]

The Mayan mythologies and shamanistic practice show a
broader and more fundamental meaning to these numbers.
The number 13 represents specific configurations of powers
or forces, with 20 being the number of elemental energies;
these forces and energies combine to form the dynamic of
life. Each individual day has its particular force and energy,
the former represented in the day's number, the latter in
the day's glyph, each of which are also associated with an
element, plant, animal or bird (*see* Table 1). The purpose of
this emphasis on forces and energies is to direct the
individual to the unique character of each day, to 'seize' the
day, to focus his consciousness on the significance of the
day, particularly birth dates, his own and those of his family
and friends. Naturally, when rightly understood, each 20-
day cycle has its own accumulating significance as does each
of their 13 repetitions through 260 days. The Maya believed
that this kind of daily consciousness connected them with
the broader rhythms and vibrations of the Earth, and all of
life. The same is true of each block of time computed from
these two numbers. The Tzolk'in, rightly understood and
used, is a tool or mechanism that aids the process of our

necessary integration with Nature and the rhythms of the cosmos. This is a leitmotif of the prophecies (*see*, for example, Prophecies 3, 5, 12 and 16).

The Tzolk'in was the means by which the Maya kept track of the cycles of the Pleiades, a constellation of considerable significance to them. They called it 'Tzab' which means, in Yucatec Mayan, 'rattle', understood to be the tail of the 'rattlesnake' constellation. During 2012, there will be two eclipses of the Sun, the first being on 20 May when the Sun and Moon will conjunct with the Pleiades; the second eclipse will occur on 13 November when the Sun and Moon will conjunct with the constellation Serpens, the Serpent. These two eclipses are the physical mark of the cosmic orobouros, the primordial serpent, the snake swallowing its own tail (*see* Prophecy 6).

It was by combining the Haab and Tzolk'in that the Maya constructed another of their calendars, the Calendar Round.

# APPENDIX 3

# THE CALENDAR ROUND

The Calendar Round is constructed by combining and interlocking the Haab and the Tzolk'in cycles so as to produce a new cycle of 52 years.

*This is the Calendar, the summation of the years or Calendar Round. This array of years is continuous to its expected completion. ...*
*Then it repeats over and over forever. ...*
*This is the truth.*

**Chilam Balam of Tizimin [138]**

The Calendar Round is of great antiquity; as well as representing aspects of Mayan cosmology, it existed throughout Mesoamerican societies, probably since c.2500 BCE. Its development has been traced from the Zapotec, through the Olmec, and thus to the Maya.

The calendar is constructed from a combination of the 365-day solar Haab and the 260-day count of the Tzolk'in cycle. The 365 days of the solar year are cycled 260 times in exactly the same way in which the 20 days of the Tzolk'in are cycled 13 times. This gives a total combination of 18,980 days, (being the lowest common multiple of 260 and 365) or 73 Tzolk'in (260-day) cycles. Another, perhaps clearer, way of thinking of this is as a cycle of 52 years before the first day of the year recurs as the first day of the 260-day cycle.

Neither the Haab, nor the Tzolk'in calendars actually numbered the years, but the 52-year cycle was sufficient to provide a calendar that could identify specific days and months or other periods of time, and which lasted for the duration of most people's lives. The Calendar Round was not only used by the Maya, but also by the Toltec and the later Aztecs. The end of the Calendar Round cycle was particularly significant, and thought to be an unsettled period of darkness and unrest in much the same way as the 5-day Wayeb. The Maya waited anxiously to see if another cycle of 52 years would be given to them by the gods. To ensure this, various rituals were performed such as the New Fire ceremony (*see* Introduction), the adding of a new level to pyramids and temples, and by carving inscriptions on monuments and steles.

The Calendar Round is frequently illustrated by showing two intermeshing gears, the smaller one representing the Tzolk'in, the larger the Haab.

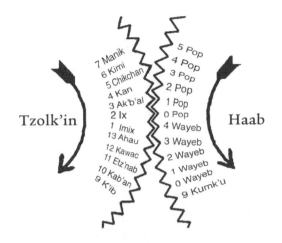

Tzolk'in

7 Manik
6 Kimi
5 Chikchan
4 Kan
3 Ak'b'al
2 Ix
1 Imix
13 Ahau
12 Kawac
11 Etz'nab
10 Kab'an
9 K'ib

5 Pop
4 Pop
3 Pop
2 Pop
1 Pop
0 Pop
4 Wayeb
3 Wayeb
2 Wayeb
1 Wayeb
0 Wayeb
9 Kumk'u

Haab

The intermeshed cogs show how the two calendars combine. Each cog of the wheel on the left carries one of the Tzolk'in's 20 day names for the full 260-day cycle. The larger, right-hand wheel has 365 cogs, and their interstices carry the names of every day of the 365-day Haab year. In this illustration the Tzolk'in's 2 Ix is placed in conjunction with the Haab's *0 Pop*, the latter marking the beginning of the Haab year, the former one of the days on which the Tzolk'in 260-day cycle can start. Suggested 'start' days are called 'year-bearers'. However, it is argued that the Tzolk'in is truly circular and, thus, has no start or end date.[139]

In the above illustration, as the Tzolk'in wheel on the left is rotated, the Haab wheel on the right will rotate in the opposite direction, thus the cogs will show the conjunction of the days of both calendars throughout the cycle. As noted, it will take a cycle of 52 years for the first day of the Haab to coincide, again, with the first day of the Tzolk'in, which in its turn will need to cycle 73 times. Thus for the Haab it is 52 x 365 days, and for the Tzolk'in it is 73 x 260 days. Both, therefore, amount to the same period of 18,980 days. These cycles were naturally written out in the form of tables covering the whole of the 52 years. This period is sometimes referred to as the Maya or Aztec century, even though 'half-century' would be more appropriate, but 'Calendar Round' is the most frequently used name.

Because of the conjunction of the two calendars, every day in the cycle will have two ways of being recorded, since each will have two names (as shown in the illustration of the cog-wheels): that of the Tzolk'in, or the Day Count calendar, and that of the Haab, the Solar calendar. Each day and each month also have their own glyphs with alternatives and variants, and the complexity faced by scholars when interpreting inscriptions can readily be understood.

At this point it would be useful to summarize the calendric building blocks discussed above:

* The Tun is made up of 18 months, each of 20 days, creating a 'vague' year of 360 days.
* The Haab is a 365-day solar year, divided into the eighteen 20-day months of the Tun, with a final short month of 5 days.
* The Tzolk'in is a period of 20 days cycled by 13, giving a 260-day period for the cycle to be completed.
* The Calendar Round, or Great Cycle, is a combination of the Haab and the Tzolk'in, and takes a period of 18,980 days, or 52 years, for its own cycle to be completed.

We can now add to this, the last of the most important of the Mayan calendars.

# APPENDIX 4

# THE LONG COUNT CALENDAR

*The Long Count Start Glyph*

(The glyph means 'the completion of 13 *baktuns*'. The *baktun*, *katun*, *tun*, *winal* and *kin*, also have their own glyphs.)

The Long Count Calendar, or Great Cycle, covers a period of approximately 5,126 years. The current period started on 13 August 3114 BCE and will end on 21 December 2012. This end date is now approaching rapidly, and because the calendric prophecies are pointing to this date, it is attracting increasing world-wide interest.

*Could there come a time when the magic
drawing of the days should cease? The sacred
Long Count shall be kept in order by magic
enduring to the end!*

**Chilam Balam of Tizimin**

*The Maya conceived of the Great Cycle as one
World Age, one growth cycle, at the end of
which humanity reaches the next stage of its
spiritual development. According to calendric
science, the Great Cycle times our collective
unfolding as a species, as well as the cycles of
culture*[140]

The Long Count Calendar was kept during the Classical
period of the Maya, c.300–900 CE. Its oldest inscription,
dated 36 BCE, was found at Chiapa de Corzo, on Stele 2, but
it is recorded in several other inscriptions. Like the Haab,
the Long Count Calendar, in having a specific beginning
and end, appears to represent the traditional linear concept
of time. As a construct it enabled the Maya to record history,
to organize the present and to plan the future, but, as we
shall see, it forms the basis for an alternative perception of

time. Stephen Hawking has explained that relativity requires us to abandon our long-held notion of time being a fixed, isolated dimension, and that it is inextricably related to space.[141] Because time recurs, turns and loops back in on itself unendingly, it is no longer possible to think of it as something that can be measured definitively. It is this cyclic notion of time, the concept of recurrence and return that provides the framework for the prophecies.

As noted on p.212 the Long Count Calendar began on 13 August 3114 BCE, and ends with the winter solstice of 21 December 2012, a period of 5,126 years, alternatively referred to as the 'Great Cycle'. The start-date was determined by using a standard method of correlating dates found inscribed on steles and pyramids with the Julian and Gregorian calendars. The start-date of the Long Count Calendar, 13 August 3114 BCE, called also the 'Birth of Venus', is the one generally accepted by scholars, but this is debated by some.[142] While numerous methods have been proposed for calculating date correlations, most of them are only of historical interest. The correlation used most frequently is the so-called Goodman-Martinez-Thompson (GMT) method that has been corroborated by the University of Pennsylvania's extensive carbon dating of sapodilla wood beams that the ancient Maya used to span temple doorways.[143] The correlation is based on calculating the proleptic Gregorian calendar back through the Julian dates, that is, extending its date-pattern backwards from its introduction in 1582 CE.

The end of the Long Count Calendar, 21 December 2012, calculated by the GMT correlation, is consistent with the archaeological and historical evidence carved in inscriptions, and with the continued use of the Long Count Calendar by the Quiché of today. From any sure date in the Gregorian calendar a correlation can be made with Mayan calendric dates working both forwards and backwards throughout the 5,126 years of the current Great Cycle. In this way, from the inscriptions of dates and records of the surviving codices, the generally accepted start-date of the Long Count Calendar is, indeed, 13 August 3114 BCE. There are now computer programmes available that will provide the correlation either way, between dates on the Gregorian or Long Count Calendar. Even though only one date in one calendric system needs to be securely established with one date in the other system, this start-date might seem to be arbitrary, but scholars are agreed that it fits the astronomical, ethnographic, carbon-dating and historical data. In the same way, the end date is worked forward, from the start-date, for the prescribed number of 13 *baktuns*. Between these two dates is what amounts to a 'count of days', broken down into specific units of time of the kind we have already considered. They can be simply represented as follows:

## TABLE 4: THE LONG COUNT CALENDAR'S UNITS OF TIME USING THE YUCATEC NAMES

| Number of Days | The Long Count Period | The Accumulating Time | Number of Solar Years | Tuns |
|---|---|---|---|---|
| 1 | = 1 *kin* | | | |
| 20 | = 20 *kins* | = 1 *winal* | | |
| 360 | = 18 *winals* | = 1 *tun* | ~ 1 | 1 |
| 7,200 | = 20 *tun* | = 1 *katun* | ~ 20 | 20 |
| 144,000 | = 20 *katuns* | = 1 *baktun* | ~ 395 (394.3) | 400 |

We can see from this that the *tun* is based on 360 *kins*, the Haab, on 365 *kins*, broken down into 18 *winals* with the 5 dreaded *kins* of the Wayeb added; that the Tzolk'in comprises a period of 1 *winal*, cycled 13 times, and that 18 *winals* (360 *kins*) or a *tun*, approximates to the length of a year. The new, and very significant units, are the 20-*tun* period, called a *katun* and the 20-*katun* period called a *baktun*. The 5,126 years of the Long Count Calendar are made up of very nearly 13 *baktuns* (12.8) which with the 20-*tun* and 20-*katun* periods continues the use of the 'sacred' numbers 13 and 20 (*see above*).

The present Great Cycle comprises 13 *baktuns*, and the next cycle, or new era will start following 21 December 2012, so we are now in the final *katun* (20 years) of the last of the 13 *baktuns* of the present era. There are also names for very much longer period of times, for example, 1 *pictun* = 20 *baktuns* = 2, 888,000 days = approximately 7,885 years. At 63 million years, the *alautun* is the longest named period of any known calendar. However, these longer periods are very rarely used.

In the Long Count, a Mayan date is indicated by the number of each of these units of time advancing from the given start-date, following the order: *baktun, katun, tun, winal* and *kin*. Thus, the first day of the start-date was inscribed in the generally accepted correlation as 0 : 0: 0: 0: 0. Since a cycle of nearly 13 *baktuns* will have taken place by the time we get to 21 December 2012, the end date is inscribed as 13: 0: 0: 0: 0. In some records the numbers are reversed showing the Long Count as a countdown rather than a count-up. As with all the other units of time, those of the Long Count Calendar have their glyphs which were carved on the surfaces of monuments and steles when dates were being recorded.

The present Long Count of 5,126 years is understood as only one of an indefinite number of cycles. When the current cycle ends on 21 December 2012, the new cycle will begin as 1: 0: 0: 0: 0. The Maya considered the end of a *baktun* to be the start of a new era and similarly the end of a 20-year period, or *katun*, was also significant. The *katun* length of 20 years was determined by fixed dates in much the same way as our own decades or centuries, and were the units of time most suitable for recording the length of a ruler's reign, some of which could last for upwards of three *katuns*.

The innumerable important dates carved in stone on the faces of monuments, pyramids and steles use the forms of dates shown above, plus the Haab and Tzolk'in dates. I am typing this on 1 March, 2007. Using the GMT correlation system, this transcribes into the Mayan date formula as 12.19.14.12.16. following the sequence, *baktun* 12: *katun* 19: *tun* 14: *winal* 12: *kin* 16, to which is added, Tzolk'in 11: Haab 4. The number of days elapsed since the Long Count Cycle started is, 1,868, 890, or approximately 5,120 years; the number of days remaining until the end of 13th *baktu*n on 21 December 2012, is roughly 2,055, or just over 5 years. The total, in years, thus approximates to the 5,126 years of the current cycle.

The *katun* emerges as the basic unit of time. In the early 16th century, when the Spaniards arrived in the Yucatan, the longest period of time kept by the Maya was the *U kahlay katunob*, 'the count of *katuns*', being a cycle of 13 *katuns*, amounting, as we have seen, to approximately 260 years. This is sometimes referred to as the Short Count Calendar, to distinguish it from the Long Count, and it was this that was used to record events in the post-Classical period, that is, from c.900 CE. The *katun* is named from its final date in the Tzolk'in, and as the cycle comprises 20 days and 13 numbers, the mathematics determines that a *katun* will always end on the day Ahau, one of 1 Ahau to 13 Ahau. The *katun* name is, therefore, always Ahau, preceded by its number. 'Ahau' means 'Lord', and in the mythology each of the series of 13 *katuns* has a lord. Schele[*] has suggested that these lords have astronomical names, representing events that have occurred during the *katuns* over which they rule for the 20-year period. In Roys' translation of the *katun* prophecies, the lords are illustrated:

> We have here a picture of the thirteen Lords of the Katuns. The blurred faces may signify that they are blindfolded. The crowns, crosses and manner of drawing are purely European, but they doubtless represent the idols set up in honour of each *katun*. Unfortunately no pre-Conquest representation of these figures has come down to us.[144]

At the time of the Spanish Conquest, Chilam Balam of Chumayel mourned the inability to celebrate the rites of one of these lords, because of the killing of the priests who kept the calendars:

How can the generations of the sons of the Itza tell us the days of the prophecies and the days of the *tun*? How can we celebrate the rites of Lord 5 Ahau in the twelfth *tun*, when he comes in benign holiness ... in Katun 5 Ahau, in the twelfth *tun*?[145]

# APPENDIX 5

# THE VENUS CYCLE

The *katun* which both opens and closes the current Grand Cycle saw a transit of Venus. The Dresden Codex refers to the start-date of the Long Count Calendar as the 'Birth of Venus'. 'The Prophecy of Venus' (*see* Prophecy 9) speaks of the transit of Venus in June 2012 as both the sign for the birth of a new form, or level, of transforming consciousness and the first stage of a precessional galactic synchronization that reaches its conclusion at the winter solstice of 2012.

*The sight of Venus on the Sun is by far the noblest that astronomy can afford.*

Edmund Halley, 1691

Although Venus was of particular importance to the Maya, there is evidence that calendars were developed to record the year cycles of several other planets, including Mars, Mercury and Jupiter. Venus was not the love goddess familiar to the West, but a threatening and dangerous male deity associated with war, and in Mayan mythology it holds much the same place as did Mars in Western mythology.

The calculations based on the cycles of Venus were used to establish the auspicious dates for the coronations of kings and for planning a war, the first attack of which was always timed to coincide with the planet's ascension. There were superstitions regarding the maleficent effects of rays of light from Venus, and chinks in the structure of houses and other buildings were sealed so as to omit them. The Maya were able to calculate the cycle with extraordinary accuracy and several pages of the Dresden Codex are given up to it. The period of time it takes for the Earth, the Sun and Venus to return to a specific conjunction was calculated as 584 days; modern astronomic science has calculated the time as, 593.92 days. The Maya were very close. Five Venus years are the same as eight solar years, each having 2,902 days; it is the conjunctions of the Venus and solar years that are the subject of the tables of the Dresden and Grolier Codices.

Of the various aspects of Venus recorded in the calendars, it is the transits that particularly interested the

Maya. A transit occurs when Venus is seen to cross the face of the Sun, caused by the planet passing between the Sun and the Earth, thus obscuring a tiny part of the Sun's surface. The planet is visible as a black disk moving across part of the Sun's face, its passage taking several hours.

As well as its association with war, the phases of Venus were read as figuring death and rebirth. In mythology the planet is linked with Quetzalcoatl who returns to the underworld during the eight-day gap between the disappearance of Venus as the evening star, and its reappearance as the morning star. In the morning, Venus always precedes the Sun and can be said to be leading the god out of the underworld of the night, into a new day. In the evenings the planet is visible just after sunset when it can be understood as following the god into the underworld.

Calleman makes the intriguing suggestion that Venus is our 'sister' planet, or 'the mirror of the Earth'. The thesis is based on similarities between the rotations of both planets, indicating that in the time between two Venus passages, Venus will rotate 365 times around its own axis, that being the number of days in an Earth year. This, of course, may be a statistical coincidence, or it may be, as Calleman hints:

> a type of primal synchronicity which is linked to
> the fact that Venus has been created as the mirror

of the Earth, and maybe in the year 2012, as our consciousness has become more cosmic, this will simply be seen by us as self-explanatory.[146]

Martineau, interested in coincidences, points out that:

> Venus rotates extremely slowly on her own axis in the opposite direction to most rotations in the solar system. Her day is precisely two-thirds of an Earth year, a musical fifth. This exactly harmonizes ... so that every time Venus and Earth kiss, Venus does so with the same face looking at the Earth.[147]

Pinchbeck presents this 'coincidence' in terms of numbers in the Fibonacci sequence: *Eight Earth years equals, exactly, thirteen Venus years, the five kisses between them crafting a perfect pentagon, carved out of space. The numbers 5, 8, and 13, belong to the Fibonacci sequence, defining phi,* or the golden ratio, itself a blueprint for organic growth.[148]

That the Maya were undoubtedly aware of this is made clear from the data in the codices recording the movements of Venus.

The next transit of Venus will take place on 6 June 2012, forming part of a unique astronomical conjunction that will culminate with the winter solstice on 21 December (*see* Prophecy 9).

# APPENDIX 6

# THE MOON CALENDAR,
# OR TUN-UC

We do not have much information about the Maya's understanding of the Moon. Roys' tells us that, in the later mythologies, it was associated with the rabbit, a symbol of drunkenness, and with Tlacolteotl, the goddess of sinful love. What is important is that the form of Western calendars, with 12 lunar months per year, is out of phase with 'natural time', which is more accurately measured by a 13-month year (*see* Prophecy 20).

*Now we shall tell of the dawning and the appearance of the Sun, Moon, and stars.... There were not many people then ... There were only a few on the top of the mountain of Hacavitz. There it was the Sun, Moon and stars truly appeared. Everything on the face of the Earth and beneath the sky had its dawn and became clear.*

Popul Vuh

While the Moon and the Sun played the leading roles in the drama of the Popul Vuh creation myth, the Maya had problems in coordinating the lunar and solar calendars, that is, the period of the Moon's orbit around the Earth with the Earth's orbit around the Sun. The calendar that attempted this rationalization was called the Tun-Uc. '*Tun*' means 'count,' and '*Uc*' means both 'Moon' and 'seven'. The 'seven' is unclear, except that it relates to the 7-day week of the Gregorian calendar, and thus to the 4 weeks of the unmanageable 28-day month. The 12 synodic lunar months of 29.53 days, amounts to 354.36 days, virtually 11 days short of the 365 days of the solar year. Coe points out that:

> despite their 'Vague' year and lack of intercalation, the Maya had an unusually accurate idea of the real length of the Tropical, or Seasonal Year.[149]

Numerous Long Count inscriptions are supplemented with glyphs, know as the Lunar Series. There are eight Lunar Series glyphs, and they record a date in the lunar calendar, the name of the current lunar month, indicating its length at either 29 or 30 days, and the number of days elapsed since the new Moon. These glyphs kept track of the Moon's age and changing phases, and aimed to give some fixed form to the 'erratic' Moon year. The period of the synodical, or lunar month is calculated from new Moon to new Moon and averages 29.5 days in length. However, the records alternate the lunar months of 29 and 30 days in an attempt to coordinate the lunar calendar with the phases of the Moon. In fact, the Maya abandoned any systematic attempt at a rational coordination of the cycles of the Sun and the Moon. With a hint of frustration, The Book of Chilam Balam of Tizimin [150] records that '*Yaxum our forefather cast aside the divisions of the katun pertaining to the Moon*', but in this context, '*katun*' should be read as 'calendar'. The Maya, therefore, made separate records of the Sun's movements and the Moon's irregular phases, knowing the Moon's age in days on any specific day of the month and where this conjuncted with the cycle of Venus.

Currently, two different calendar systems are offered as alternatives to the Gregorian form. One is the traditional calendar system we have met as the Tzolk'in; this is still in use in some regions of Guatemala, and as described above, it is an interlocking part of the prophetic Long Count Calendar of 13 *baktuns*. It is possible to read the Long Count Calendar as the Tzolk'in written large, or magnified, the latter containing in concentrated form all the energies of the former. The other alternative is the so-called 'Dreamspell' calendar introduced by Argüelles, who rightly points out that every time the Earth goes round the Sun, the Moon goes round the Earth 13 times.[151] Nature, Argüelles plausibly argues, has therefore given us a perfectly natural base for a 13-Moon calendar, a concept he calls 'natural time'. Dreamspell is attracting considerable attention as an alternative calendar, but it is entirely spurious to suppose that the 13-Moon calendar is simply a modernized form of the traditional Mayan calendar. To specify, and explain at length, the marked differences between these alternatives is beyond the scope of this book, but it has to be kept in mind that the Tzolk'in is inextricably related to the Long Count Calendar, and Dreamspell is not; that the traditional calendars record and describe an ongoing process of cosmic rhythms and relationships, and form the basis of the prophetic tradition, whereas Dreamspell simply offers a new way of dividing the solar year. While Argüelles' suggestion is important, and should be taken into consideration in its own right, it cannot be read as a replacement, or displacement, of the tradition. This significant theme has been developed and discussed as Prophecy 20.

# LAST WORD

## SUMMARY OF APPENDICES

The Mayan understanding of time is made concrete in the structures of their various calendars. Trying to understand how the calendars work, and how they represent cycles of time over long periods, is something of a mechanical process, allied to complicated mathematics. The interlinking of the Haab and Tzolk'in calendars to form the Calendar Round, and their combined relationship in the Long Count Calendar, presents a concept of time radically different from our own. For the Maya, time was cyclic, and it is this perception that provides the context for a prophetic tradition that was a way of life. In refuting a linear concept of time, the Maya turned away from a dominating materialism. The alternative, cyclic concept of time offers both an insight to an aspect of consciousness of which, for the moment, we in the West have little perception (*see* Prophecies 13 and 20).

# REFERENCES

*(See* Further Reading, *under authors, for details of the books.)*

| | | | |
|---|---|---|---|
| 1. | Gallenkamp | 22. | Roys 1 |
| 2. | Reading | 23. | Roys 1 |
| 3. | Coe 2 | 24. | Roys 2 |
| 4. | Christenson | 25. | Roys 2 |
| 5. | Miller and Taube | 26. | Roys 1 |
| 6. | Miller and Taube | 27. | Hunbatz Men 3 |
| 7. | Christenson | 28. | Stockbauer |
| 8. | Hunbatz Men 1 | 29. | Hunbatz Men 3 |
| 9. | Capra | 30. | Yaxk'in |
| 10. | Florescano | 31. | Hunbatz Men 3 |
| 11. | Tedlock | 32. | Makemson |
| 12. | Makemson | 33. | Hunbatz Men 3 |
| 13. | Bolio 2 | 34. | Hunbatz Men 3 |
| 14. | Makemson | 35. | Hunbatz Men 3 |
| 15. | Roys 2 | 36. | Housden |
| 16. | Roys 1 | 37. | Makemson |
| 17. | Makemson | 38. | Roys 1 |
| 18. | Bonewitz | 39. | Roys 2 |
| 19. | Roys 1 | 40. | Yaxk'in |
| 20. | Makemson | 41. | Tozzer |
| 21. | Coe 2 | 42. | Hunbatz Men 1 |

94. Napier & Wickramasinghe

95. Barrios

96. Calleman

97. Makemson

98. Pinchbeck

99. Chardin

100. Barrios

101. Oxlaj

102. Hunbatz Men 3

103. NASA

104. Gilbert

105. Gilbert

106. Hunbatz Men 5

107. Jenkins

108. *European Journal of Human Genetics*

109. Miller

110. Jenkins

111. Devi, Mataji Nirmala

112. Roys 1

113. Singularity Watch

114. Kurzweil

115. Dalai Lama

116. Birch

117. Heidegger

118. Argüelles 2

119. Makemson

120. Argüelles 2 & 3

121. Capra

122. Dogen Zenji

123. Argüelles 3

124. Argüelles 2

125. Tedlock

126. Capra

127. Roys 1

128. Jung 2

129. Argüelles

130. Wilcock

131. Lovelock

132. Williams, Dr Rowan

133. Govinda, Lama

134. Jaspers

135. Tarnas

136. Longhena

137. Jenkins

138. Makemson

139. Makemson

140. Jenkins

141. Hawking

142. Argüelles 1

# FURTHER READING

Achalananda,

'Kriya Yoga: Spiritual Science for an Awakening
Age', in *A World in Transition*, Self-Realization
Fellowship, Los Angeles, 1999

Argüelles, José,

1. *Time and the Technosphere*, Bear and Co. Rochester,
2002

2. *The Mayan Factor*, Bear and Co. Rochester, 1996

3. José Argüelles/Valum Votan, Galactic Research
Institute of the Foundation for the Law of Time
(www.lawoftime.org)

Barrios, Carlos,

1. In interview Mitch Battros on Earth Changes TV,
31 January, 2005

2. *Kam Wuj, The Book of Destiny*, Editorial
Sudamericana, Buenos Aires, 2000

Birch, Charles,

*A Purpose for Everything: Religion in Post-modern
World View*, Twentythird Publications, 1990

Bohr, Niels,

*Essays on Atomic Physics and Human Knowledge*, Wiley
Interscience, 1987, Ox Box

Boissière, Robert,

*The Return of Pahana*, Bear and Co. 1990

Bolio, Antonio Mediz,

    1. *The Land of Pheasant and Deer*, Ediciones Dante,
    S.A., Mexico City, 1983

    2. *The Books of Chilam Balam of Chumayel*, Trans. E-
    version, Suzanne D Fisher.
    http://myweb.cableone.net/

Bonewitz, Dr Ronald

    *Maya Prophecy*, Piatkus, 1999

Broglie, Louis de,

    *Researches on Quantum Theory*, Gauthier-Villars,
    Paris, 1924

Calleman, Carl Johan,

    *The Mayan Calendar and the Transformation of
    Consciousness*, Bear and Company, 2004

Capra, Fritjof,

    *The Tao of Physics*, Flamingo, 1992

Chase, Arlen F and Rice, Prudence M,

    *The Lowland Maya Postclassic*, University of Texas
    Press, Austin, 1995

Christenson, Allen, Trans.

    *Popul Vuh, The Sacred Book of the Maya*, University
    of Oklahoma Press, 2007

Coe, Michael D.

    1. *Breaking the Maya Code*, Thames and Hudson, 1992

    2. *The Maya*, Thames and Hudson, 1997

Coe, Michael and Van Stone, Mark,

    *Reading the Maya Glyphs*, Thames and Hudson, 2001

CPWR: Council for a Parliament of World Religions:
http://www.cpwr.org

Dalai Lama, quoted in,

*Gentle Bridges: Conversations with the Dalai Lama on the Sciences of Mind*, Jeremy Hayward and Francisco Varela. Shambala, 1992

Davis, Joel,

*Journey to the Center of our Galaxy*, Contemporary Books, Chicago, 1991

Dawkins, Richard,

*The Selfish Gene*, Penguin Books, 1976

De Chardin, Pierre Teilhard,

*The Phenomenon of Man*, Collins, Fount Paperback, 1959

Devi, Mataji Nirmala, Shri,

Address to the Inter-regional Round Table Fourth World Conference on Women, Beijing, September 13, 1995

Dogen Zenji,

*Enlightenment Unfolds*, Kazuaki Tanahashi (ed), Shambhala Publications Inc., U.S., 2000

Drew, David,

*The Lost Chronicles of the Maya Kings*, University of California Press, 1999

Edmondson, M,

*The Ancient Future of the Itza*, University of Texas Press, 1982

*European Journal of Human Genetics*, March, 2006,
    published on-line
Fernbank Science Centre, http://fsc.fernbank.edu/
Florescano, Enrique,
    *The Myth of Quetzalcoatl*, John Hopkins University
    Press, 2002
Gallenkamp, Arthur Charles,
    *Maya, The Riddle and Rediscovery of a Lost Civilization*,
    Frederick Muller Ltd. London, 1960
Geertz, Armin,
    *The Invention of Prophecy*, University of California,
    1994
Gilbert, Adrian,
    *The End of Time. The Mayan Prophecies Revisited*,
    Mainstream Publishing, Edinburgh, 2006
Gilbert, Adrian and Cotterell, Maurice,
    *The Mayan Prophecies*, Element, 1995
Govinda, Lama Anagarika,
    *Foundations of Tibetan Mysticism*, Samuel Weiser, Inc.
    1969
Havel, Vaclav,
    *The Spiritual Roots of Democracy*, An address given to
    the Law School of Stamford University, 1994
Hawking, Stephen W,
    *A Brief History of Time*, Guild Publishing, 1990
Heidegger, Martin,
    *Being and Time*, Blackwell, 1995

Honoré, Pierre,

   *In Quest of the White God*, Hutchinson, London, 1963

Housden, Roger,

   *Sacred Journeys in a Modern World*, Simon and
   Schuster, 1998

Hunbatz Men,

   1. *Secrets of Mayan Science/Religion*, Bear and Co. 1990

   2. *Pacal Votan:* http://www.13moon.com

   3. *Mayan Prophecies for the New Millennium*,
      http://www.13moon.com

   4. 'The Sacred Manuscript of K'altun', Mayan
      Initiation Centres, Mérida Yucatan, Mexico

   5. 'Initiation in the Mayan Consciousness', at the
      Prophets Conference, Victoria, B.C. Canada, 2001

James, William,

   *The Varieties of Religious Experience*, Signet Classics,
   2003

Jaspers, Karl,

   *Way to Wisdom*, Yale University Press, 2003

Jelusich, Richard, at www.lightnews.org

Jenkins, John Major,

   *Maya Cosmogenesis 2012*, Bear and Company,
   Rochester, 1998

Jung, C J,

   1. *Memories, Dreams, Reflections*, Collins, Fount
      Paperback, 1963

   2. *The Undiscovered Self*, Routledge, UK, 1990

Kurzweil, Ray,

*The Age of Spiritual Machines: When Computers Exceed Human Intelligence*, Penguin Books, 1999

Laughton, Timothy,

*The Maya: Life, Myth and Art*, Duncan Baird Publishers, 1998

Léon-Portilla, Miguel, Ed.

*Native Mesoamerican Spirituality*, SPCK, 1980

Longhena, Maria,

*Maya Script*, Abbeville Press, 2000

Looff, Roland de, *see* Acknowledgements

Love, Bruce,

*The Paris Codex, Handbook for a Maya Priest*, University of Texas Press, Austin, 1994

Lovelock, James,

*Gaia: A New Look at Life on Earth* (1979, 3rd ed. 2000) Oxford University Press

Makemson, M W, Trans.

*The Book of the Jaguar Priest, a translation of the Book of Chilam Balam of Tizimin*, Henry Schuman, New York, 1951

Martineau, John,

*A Little Book of Coincidence*, Wooden Books Ltd 2006

McFadden, Steve, founder of The Wisdom Conservancy, now a Director of Chiron Communications; (www.chiron-communications.com)

Millar, Mary and Taube, Karl,

    *An Illustrated Dictionary of The Gods and Symbols of*
    *Ancient Mexico and the Maya*, Thames and Hudson, 1993

Miller, Richard and Iona,

    *Nexus Magazine,* Volume 10, Number 3, April-May
    2003

Napier and Wickramasinghe,

    'Chance of a Comet Impact Reassessed',
    http://www.spacedaily.com/news/asteroid-040.html

NASA.gov

Oxlaj, Don Alejandro, from a speech given in Santa Fe,
    October 2005

Pacal Votan, *see* http://www.13moon.com and
    http://www.lawoftime.org/home

Paramahansa Yogananda,

    *Autobiography of a Yogi*, Rider, Random House, 1996

Peat, David F,

    *Synchronicity*, Bantam Books 1987. Quoted in
    Pinchbeck, *2012 The Year of the Mayan Prophecy*

Pinchbeck, Daniel,

    *2012, The Year of the Mayan Prophecy*, Piatkus, 2006

Reading, Mario,

  *Nostradamus: The Complete Prophecies for the Future*,
    Watkins Publishing, 2006

Rourke, Dwayne Edward, *see* http://www.dwayneed-
wardrourke.com

Roys, Ralph L, Trans.

    1. *The Book of Chilam Balam of Chumayel*, University of
       Oklahoma Press, 1967

    2. 'The Prophecies for the Maya Tuns or Years In the
       Books of Chilam Balam of Tizimin and Mani',
       *American Anthropology and History*, No.51. 1949.
       Reprinted from the Carnegie Institution of
       Washington, Publication 585, 1949

Sabloff, Jeremy and Andrews, E Wyllys,

    *Late Lowland Maya Civilisation, Classic to Post-Classic*,

    University of Mexico Press, Albuquerque, 1986

Scaruffi, Piero,

    *The Nature of Consciousness*, Omniware, 2006

Schele, Linda and Freidel, David,

    *A Forest of Kings*, Morrow & Co. New York, 1990

Schele, Linda and Peter Mathews,

    *The Code of Kings*, Touchstone, 1999

Singularity Watch, *see* at: http://www.singularity.org

Stockbauer, Bette,

    'Ancient Prophecies for Modern Times',

    http://www.bci.org/prophecy- fulfilled/ancient.htm

*Tanakh, The Holy Scriptures,* A new JPS translation according

    to the traditional Hebrew Text, The Jewish

    Publication Society, 5746/1985

Tarnas, Richard,

    *Cosmos and Psyche, Intimations of a New World View*,

    Viking, 2006

Taube, Karl,

    *Aztec and Maya Myths*, British Museum Press, 1993

Tedlock, Barbara,

    *Time and the Highland Maya*, University of New
    Mexico Press, Albuquerque, 1982

Thomson, J Eric, S,

    1. *Maya Hieroglyphic Writing*, University of Oklahoma
    Press, 1971

    2. *The Rise and Fall of Mayan Civilisation*, University of
    Oklahoma Press, 1966

    3. *Maya History and Religion*, University of Oklahoma
    Press, 1970

    4. *A Commentary on the Dresden Codex*, American
    Philosophical Society, Philadelphia, 1972

Wilcock, David,

    *The Breakthroughs of Russian Astrophysicist Dr Nikolai
    A Kozyrev*, article posted on the website
    www.divinecosmos.com.

Williams, Dr Rowan, Archbishop of Canterbury, in a
    speech given in Sri Lanka, May, 2007

Yaxk'in, Aluna Joy,

    *Mayan Prophecy: The Reawakening of Cosmic Man*
    On-line article: www.adishakti.org

Yukteswar, Swami Sri,

    *The Holy Science*, Self-Realization Fellowship,

Yogoda Satsanga Society of India, 1990